MW01121689

Nita Mehta's
BAKES & CAKES
Baking With Confidence!

Nita Mehta

M.Sc. (Food & Nutrition), Gold Medalist

CO AUTHOR
BRINDA MALIK
B.Sc. Home Science, B.Ed

SNAB
Publishers Pvt. Ltd.

Nita Mehta's
BAKES & CAKES

© Copyright 2002-2005 **SNAB** Publishers Pvt Ltd

WORLD RIGHTS RESERVED: The contents - all recipes, photographs and drawings are original and copyrighted. No portion of this book shall be reproduced, stored in a retrieval system or transmitted by any means, electronic, mechanical, photocopying, recording or otherwise, without the written permission of the publishers.

While every precaution is taken in the preparation of this book, the publishers and the author assume no responsibility for errors or omissions. Neither is any liability assumed for damages resulting from the use of information contained herein.

TRADEMARKS ACKNOWLEDGED: Trademarks used, if any, are acknowledged as trademarks of their respective owners. These are used as reference only and no trademark infringement is intended upon. Ajinomoto (monosodium glutamade, MSG) is a trademark of Aji-no-moto company of Japan. Use it sparingly if you must as a flavour enhancer.

3rd Print 2005

ISBN 81-86004-77-7

Food Styling & Photography: **SNAB**

Layout and laser typesetting:

National Information Technology Academy
3A/3, Asaf Ali Road
New Delhi-110002
☎ 23252948

Published by:

SNAB
Publishers Pvt. Ltd.
3A/3 Asaf Ali Road,
New Delhi - 110002
Tel: 23252948, 23250091
Telefax:91-11-23250091

Editorial and Marketing office:
E-159, Greater Kailash-II, N.Delhi-48
Fax: 91-11-29225218, 29229558
Tel: 91-11-29214011, 29218727, 29218574
E-Mail: nitamehta@email.com
snab@snabindia.com
*Website:*http://www.nitamehta.com
Website: http://www.snabindia.com

Picture on page 1: **Chicken & Sweet Corn**
Lasange with Minced Mutton
Apple & Date Cake
Blue Berry Cheese Cake

Picture on page 2: **Beans & Cauliflower Casserole**
Glazed Mocha Fudge Cake

Picture on cover: **Mutton Hot Pot**
Orange Chiffon Cake
Walnut & Raisin Cookies

Picture on back cover: **Carrot & Date Cake**
Hot Chocolate Souffle

Picture on last page: **Chicken with Olives & Tomatoe**
Peach Trifle

Printed at:
BRIJBASI ART PRESS LTD.

Distributed by :
THE VARIETY BOOK DEPOT
A.V.G. Bhavan, M 3 Con Circus,
New Delhi - 110 001
Tel : 23417175, 23412567; Fax : 23415335
Email: varietybookdepot@rediffmail.com

Price: Rs. 189/-

Introduction

$\mathcal{W}$hether you are looking for a baked dish to serve a family meal or something special to choose for a party, there are lots of ideas for you! "Bakes & Cakes" will help you perfect savoury dishes like quick *cabbage rolls smothered with a sweet and sour tomato sauce, spinach bakes* with different combinations like potatoes, mushrooms or corn,  *eggplant bakes* and so many others. The non vegetarian recipes like *fish baked with chutney, chicken with olives and tomatoes and mutton hot pot* will make your family and friends want to have them over and over again.

The book will also help you master *truffle cake, banana walnut cake, fancy party cakes, cookies* and many baked desserts and puddings. The *apple crumble, baked cheese cake* and *orange & pineapple meringue* make wonderful desserts.

A variety of eggless cakes, especially the *raisin cake,* are a welcome change for the egg eaters and will surely turn out to be prized recipes for the non- egg eaters. If a delicious pie is your goal, the book will take you step by step through the 'blind' baking of the shell, preparing the fragrant filling and then assembling the whole thing together.

All recipes are quick and simple to prepare but still give delicious results. The list of ingredients for a particular recipe is not too long, to put you off the mood to bake. We hope that you'll take pleasure in the process and the many wonderful results!

Nita Mehta

ABOUT THE RECIPES

MEASURING CUP (240 ml)

For baking a perfect cake the right measurements are very important. So, a measuring cup of 240 ml (8 oz) has been used to try out all the recipes in the book.

Contents

BAKED DISHES & SNACKS   13

VEGETARIAN

NON-VEGETARIAN

Mushrooms & Macaroni in Spinach
Sesame Sauce   45
Baked Vegetable Rosti   46
Greens Baked with Corn   47
Vegetable Au Gratin   48
Shredded Spinach Bake   50
Florets in Broccoli Sauce   52
Rice Aubergine Casserole   53
Crepes Florentine   56
Italian Tomatoes   57
Mushroom Wraps   58
Sweet & Sour Cabbage   60
Home made Crusty Pizza   61
Calzone   62
Onion & Capsicum Hot Dogs   63
Corn & Mushroom Quiche   64

Baked Lemon Chicken   34
Garlic Onion Cheese Flan   51
Potato Nests   54
Crunchy Baked Fish   55
Tomato Fish   55
Chicken Parcels   65
Chilly Chicken Pizza   66

TEA TIME CAKES   67

WITHOUT-EGGS

Raisin Cake   78
Quick Iced Chocolate Cake   80
Marble Cake   81
Orange Cup Cake   82
Yogurt Chocolate Cake   82
Fruit Bar   83

WITH-EGGS

Coffee Cake   68
Banana Walnut Cake   70
Apple & Date Cake   71
Cardamom Cake   72
Cherry Almond Cake   73
Carrot & Date Cake   74
Orange Marmalade Cake   75
Low Fat - Yogurt Cake   76
Dark Chocolate Cake   77

FANCY PARTY CAKES   84

Pink Silver Cup Cakes   85
Glazed Mocha Fudge Cake   86
Date & Nut Loaf with Toffee Sauce   87
Fresh Fruit Gateau   88
Chocolate Truffle   90
Foot Ball Cake   92

Orange Chiffon Cake   93
Chocolate Temptation   94
Hawaiian Cake   96
Basic Sponge Cake   97
Black Forest Cake   98

COOKIES, PIES, TARTS & SWEET SNACKS   100

WITHOUT-EGGS

Chocolate Chip Cookies   101
Cashewnut Cookies   103
Cumin Cookies   103
Chocolate Glace Cookies   104
Chocolate Sesame Cookies   104
Fresh Fruit Tarts   105
Apple Roll   106
Choco Truffle Tarts   107
Date & Walnut Pie   108

WITH-EGGS

Walnut Brownies   101
Walnut & Raisin Cookies   102
Coconut Macaroons   102
Peanut Macaroons   102
Apple Short Cake   110
Swiss Rolls with Chocolate   111

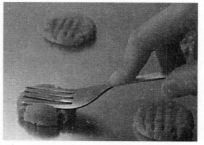

BAKED DESSERTS & PUDDINGS   112

WITHOUT-EGGS

Baked Pineapple with Fruity Caramel Sauce   113
Baked Guavas with Cream   117
Black Currant Pudding   119
Apple Crumble   120
Baked Cheese Cake with Vanilla Sauce   122
Um Ali   123
Striped Chocolate Cheese Cake   124

WITH-EGGS

Hot Chocolate Souffle   114
Blue Berry Cheese Cake   115
Crumb Delight with Rum   116
Sticky Toffee Pudding   118
Bread Pudding   121
Orange & Pineapple Meringues   121
Sponge Fruit Pudding   125
Peach Trifle   126

Baking Know How

$\mathcal{P}$lan and organize before starting to bake. Remember to preheat the oven to the temperature at which you need to bake. It is important to understand your oven. Sometimes the food gets done from outside, before it gets cooked from inside, so in such cases, reduce the temperature after a while. The same principle which is followed for foods cooked on the gas stove, holds good for the oven baked dishes too. The food baked in the centre of the oven produces the best results. Never keep the food too close to the heating coils as the food might get burnt or over done from the top.

Electrical appliances are of additional help specially an electric hand beater is excellent for mixing a cake batter. A kitchen weighing scale is very useful for correct weighing of ingredients, although for most of the recipes, the American cup will work well. A pair of common kitchen scissors are a useful accessory which can be invaluable for trimming the edges of pastry, for snipping spring onions, chopping

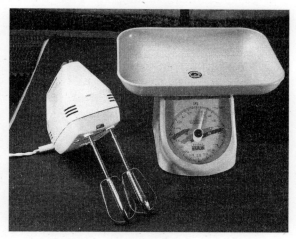

coriander and cutting fish fillets into strips and for lots of similar tasks.

In the recipes given in this book, yellow butter — Amul or Britannia has been used. The butter should be softened before measuring to avoid air pockets in the measured butter. The baking powder should always be fresh. To judge the freshness of the baking powder, drop a pinch in a glass of water. If it bubbles, the baking powder is fresh. Sometimes the fish has a peculiar fishy smell. Rub salt and turmeric on the fish and keep aside for 1-2 hours. Wash and proceed.

For the recipes given in this book, both for solid and liquid measurements, an American cup of 8 oz. (250 ml) has been used. All spoon measures given in this book are level unless otherwise stated.

Bake A Perfect Cake ... Useful Tips

★ Have all ingredients at room temperature for best results.

★ Measure/weigh the ingredients accurately.

★ Sift dry ingredients well, so that the mixture is aerated.

★ Use the correct size cake tin.

★ Prepare the cake tin before beginning to mix the cake. Grease tin lightly and dust with flour, tapping out any surplus. If the cake requires long baking, grease tin and then line with butter paper/greased brown paper. In case you are using a loose bottom tin, do remember to line it with greased butter or brown paper to prevent the batter from leaking. For sponge cakes, do not line tins with paper or else the cake will have a moist, crustless appearance.

★ Do not beat the batter after the flour has been added or the finished cake will turn out heavy.

★ Sometimes the cake batter may appear too thick even though you may have measured the ingredients very carefully, as stated in the recipe. In such cases, you may conveniently add 2-4 tbsp of milk to make the batter softer.

★ If flavouring extracts (essences) are used, add them to the fat because fat absorbs flavour readily.

★ Fill the cake tin only half to two-thirds full of batter, leaving enough space for it to rise.

★ To get a cake with a level top — scoop out a little batter from the centre to form a small depression and shift it to the sides, before putting the cake in the oven.

★ Place tin in the centre of the oven, so that hot air can circulate around it.

★ For even distribution of fruit and to avoid sinking of the dried fruit, mix fruit with a little flour before adding to the cake mixture.

★ A cake is baked when it is:

— well risen and of a good colour; and feels firm and springy when pressed with the finger tips.

— a toothpick/cake tester remains clean after being inserted into the cake at the highest point.

— when no sizzling sound is heard when held fairly close to the ear in case of fruit cake.

★ When cakes are removed from the oven, wait for 10-15 minutes before removing from the tin.

★ If the cake is to be iced or frosted, wait until it has cooled to room temperature before decorating.

★ For icings — use dry and scrupulously clean utensils, always sieve icing sugar, flavour delicately and avoid strong colourings.

Why Did It Happen To My Cake?

Quality of Cake	Reasons - any one or more of the following:
HEAVY CAKE	Too little baking powder. Too much flour. Mixture (butter and sugar) not creamed enough. Flour mixed in too vigorously. Oven too slow (the cake takes too long to get done).
A DRY CAKE	Too much baking powder or flour. Not enough fat or liquid. Too long in the oven.
A SUNKEN CAKE	Too much liquid. Too much baking powder or sugar. Too little flour. Oven door slammed or cake moved during baking. Taken out from the oven too soon.
A PEAKED CAKE	Insufficient butter/oil or baking powder/soda. Too much flour. Oven temperature too high.
A BADLY CRACKED TOP	Oven too hot. Cake tin too small. Too much flour. Not enough liquid.
FRUIT SUNK TO THE BOTTOM	Fruit not properly dried and then coated with flour. Cake mixture too thin. Fruit added before adding the flour.

Commonly Used Terms

★ **Augratin:** cooked food covered with sauce, sprinkled with cheese and browned in the oven or under a grill.

★ **Baking 'blind':** to bake pastry without a filling. The pastry case is lined with foil and weighed with dried beans to avoid puffing or rising of the pastry. An easy alternative to avoid puffing, is to prick it well before putting it in the oven.

★ **Basting:** moistening the food with juices or oil to prevent it from drying.

★ **Binding:** adding a liquid, egg or melted fat to a dry mixture to hold together.

★ **Blanching:** boiling briefly either to enhance colour as in broccoli, soften as in carrots or to loosen skin as in tomatoes or almonds.

★ **Caramel:** sugar and very little water dissolved on low heat until golden brown and syrupy.

★ **Consistency:** thickness or texture of a mixture.

★ **Castor sugar:** home ground sugar is castor sugar. Icing sugar available in the market is finer in texture than castor sugar.

★ **Dropping consistency:** the consistency of cake or pudding mixture which is when a spoonful of mixture falls from a spoon within 5 seconds without shaking the spoon.

★ **Dust:** to sprinkle lightly with flour or sugar.

★ **Folding in:** mixing a light ingredient with another ingredient which is whisked well, without losing the lightness. For e.g. adding flour to whisked eggs.

★ **Garnish:** an edible sweet or savoury decoration for all type of dishes.

★ **Kneading:** working a dough firmly with the knuckles for bread or with finger tips in case of pastry until smooth and well mixed.

★ **Parboil:** to partly boil an ingredient in order to finish cooking by another method.

Oven Temperature

	°C	°F	Gas Mark
Very cool	110	225	¼
Cool	120	250	½
Moderate	160-180	325-350	3-4
Moderately Hot	190-200	375-400	5-6
Hot	220-230	425-450	7-8
Very Hot	240	475	9

BAKED DISHES
&
SNACKS

The cup used to measure both solids and liquids in the following recipes is the American measuring cup of 8 oz (250 ml). The cup has markings of ¼ cup, ½ cup, ¾ cup and also 1/3 and 2/3 cup, which makes the measuring of ingredients very easy. The measuring cup is easily available in all stores which keep kitchen equipment. In the absence of a measuring cup, a normal big sized coffee mug can be used.

Practical Conversions

AMERICAN CUP (8 OZ, 250 ML)	WEIGHT
1 cup flour	125 gm
1 cup powdered sugar	150 gm
1 cup ordinary sugar	200 gm
1 cup softened butter	250 gm
1 cup grated cheese	100 gm
1 cup oil	250 ml

To measure, place the cup on a flat surface. Fill the ingredient and then level it. For measuring butter, press the softened butter into the cup so that air spaces are forced out.

Chicken with Olives & Tomatoes

Picture on page 127   *Serves 3-4*

200 gm boneless chicken - cut into 1" pieces
12 olives
4 large tomatoes - blanched and skinned
3 tbsp oil or butter
2 flakes garlic - crushed
1 tsp salt, ½ tsp pepper
1 tsp coriander - chopped

1. In a nonstick pan, melt 1 tbsp of butter, add the chicken pieces and fry on medium heat till golden brown. Add ¼ tsp salt and ¼ tsp pepper.
2. Sprinkle about 2 tbsp water in the chicken and cook covered till the pieces are tender. Drain the left over butter if any, keep aside the chicken pieces.
3. To make the sauce, put tomatoes in hot water for 3-4 minutes. Remove skin and grind them in a liquidizer to a puree.
4. Heat 1 tbsp oil. Add garlic, add the pureed tomatoes. Cook for 5 minutes till slightly thick.
5. Add the olives and ½ tsp salt and ¼ tsp pepper or to taste. Remove from fire. Keep the sauce aside.
6. Spread ¼ of the sauce in a greased serving dish. Arrange the chicken pieces on it and pour the remaining sauce.
7. Sprinkle coriander.
8. Bake in a preheated oven at 180°C/350°F/Gas mark 4 for 10-15 minutes.

Chicken & Sweet Corn

Serves 4   *Picture on page 1*

300 gm boneless chicken or 2 chicken breasts - cut into thin slices
1½ cups milk
½ cup sweet corn kernels (fresh or tinned), see note
3 tbsp butter - softened
2 spring onions - cut white part into rings and green into thin diagonal slices
1 big sized potato - boiled & cut into ½" pieces
2 tbsp flour (maida)
½ cup grated cheese
1 tsp salt, ½ tsp pepper

1. Melt 1 tbsp of butter in a pan, add the chicken pieces and stir fry on medium heat till golden brown. Add ¼ tsp salt and ¼ tsp pepper. Remove chicken from the pan and keep aside.
2. In the same pan, melt 2 tbsp butter and add white of spring onions and potatoes and cook till onions turn soft.
3. Add the sweet corn. Mix.
4. Add flour and greens of spring onions. Mix well and cook for 2 minutes.
5. Remove from the heat and gradually add the milk.
6. Bring to boil, stirring all the time until slightly thickened and the sauce starts coating the back of the spoon. Add ½ tsp salt and ½ tsp pepper or to taste. Remove from fire.
7. Spread ¼ of the sauce in a serving dish. Arrange the chicken pieces on the sauce.
8. Pour the remaining sauce over the chicken. Sprinkle the grated cheese.
9. Bake in a preheated oven at 180°C/350°F/Gas mark 4 for 15 minutes.

Note: If using fresh corn, boil it in 2 cups water with 2 tsp sugar and 1 tsp salt and a pinch of haldi for about 5 minutes, or till soft.

Do not overboil the potato as it has to be baked also.

Beans & Cauliflower Casserole

A delightful combination of beans with cauliflower. Any other vegetable, like mushrooms or babycorns, carrots or broccoli or mixed veggies may be substituted for cauliflower.

Picture on page 2   *Serves 6*

½ cup rajmah (red kidney beans) - soaked overnight
1 onion - chopped
3 tomatoes - blanched, peeled and chopped (250 gm)
4 cups finely chopped cauliflower
2½ tbsp tomato ketchup
1 tsp Worcestershire sauce
1½ cups (150 gm) grated cheese
½ cup cream
2 tbsp oil
salt and pepper to taste

1. Pressure cook rajmah with 2 cups water and ½ tsp salt to give 1 whistle. Keep on low heat for 20 minutes or till soft.
2. Fry the onions and cauliflower in 2 tbsp oil until onions turn golden and the cauliflower is cooked. Add 1 tsp salt and ½ tsp pepper.
3. Drain the water from the cooked rajmah. Add tomatoes, rajmah, ketchup and worcestershire sauce to the onions. Mix well. Check salt and pepper.
4. Remove from fire. Add half of the grated cheese.
5. Put the mixture in a baking dish.
6. Mix the other half of the cheese with cream. Add ¼ tsp salt and ¼ tsp pepper. Pour cream over the vegetables and spread gently.
7. Cook at 180°C/350°F/Gas mark 4 for 25 minutes or till done.

Mexican Chili Con Carne

Serves 6

½ kg mutton - minced
¾ cup red kidney beans (rajmah) - soaked overnight and boiled
4 tbsp oil
1 onion - chopped, 4 flakes garlic - crushed
2 cups tomato puree
1 tsp sugar, 1 tsp salt, ½ tsp pepper
2 tsp red chilli powder

1. Heat oil, add garlic and fry for 1 minute. Add the onion and fry for another 2 minutes. Add the mince and cook for about 5-7 minutes till brown.
2. Add the tomato puree, sugar, 1 tsp salt, ½ tsp pepper and chilli powder and the boiled beans.
3. Pour the mixture in a greased casserole, cover and bake for 2 hours in a slow oven at 150°C/300°F/Gas mark 2.

Potatoes Nicoise

Serves 8

4 potatoes
4 large tomatoes
1 magie seasoning cube
100 gm grated cheese (1 cup)
2 tbsp butter - softened

1. Boil the potatoes till half done and cut into ¼" thick slices.
2. Cut the tomatoes into ¼" thick slices.
3. Butter an oven proof dish & arrange a layer of potatoes, using half the potatoes. Sprinkle some salt and pepper. Arrange a tomato layer on the potatoes and again sprinkle salt and pepper. Sprinkle some cheese. Repeat the layers again.
4. Boil ½ cup of water. Add the seasoning cube and cook till it dissolves. Cook for a few minutes till slightly thick. Pour it over the potatoes and tomatoes.
5. Sprinkle the remaining cheese and dot with butter.
6. Bake in a moderately hot oven at 200°C/400°F/Gas mark 6 for about 40 minutes until the top is golden brown.

Eggplant Parmagiana

An Italian favourite from the city of Parma in Italy.

Picture on facing page   Serves 10-12

2 eggplants of oblong round variety (bharte ke baingan)
4 cubes cheddar cheese (Britannia) or 75-100 gm mozzarella cheese
oil for frying

TOMATO SAUCE
½ kg large tomatoes - blended to a puree in a mixer
1 onion - chopped finely, 4 flakes garlic - crushed
8-10 basil or coriander leaves - finely chopped
1 tsp dried oregano, ½ tsp chilli powder, ½ tsp sugar, 1 tsp salt, or to taste
2 tbsp oil
2 tbsp tomato sauce
2 tbsp thick cream

WHITE SAUCE
2½ tbsp butter - softened
1 small onion - finely chopped
2½ tbsp plain flour (maida)
2 cups milk
1 tsp salt and ¼ tsp pepper, or to taste
2 tbsp thick cream

1. Cut the eggplants into ¼" thick round slices and spread them out on a plate. Sprinkle 1 tsp salt and rub well to salt both sides of the eggplant. Keep aside for 15 minutes. Rinse in water and pat dry on a clean kitchen towel. Deep fry in oil, turning sides, to make them light brown on both sides.

2. To prepare the white sauce, melt the butter in a heavy bottomed pan or a kadhai. Add onion and stir till it just changes colour. Sprinkle flour and cook on low heat for 1 minute without browning, stirring throughout. Remove from heat and gradually add the milk. Mix until well blended. Return to heat and cook slowly for about 5 minutes on low heat, stirring throughout until the sauce thickens and coats the spoon well. Remove from fire. Add cream, salt and pepper. Mix well.

3. For the tomato sauce, heat 2 tbsp oil and fry the onion for 2-3 minutes till it slightly changes colour. Add the tomatoes, tomato sauce, garlic and basil leaves.

contd...

Eggplant Parmagiana ➤
Mushrooms & Macaroni in Spinach Sesame Sauce : Recipe on page 45 ➤

Add 1 tsp oregano, ½ tsp chilli powder, ½ tsp sugar and 1 tsp salt. Boil for 10 minutes on low heat till the juice from the tomatoes evaporates and it turns slightly thick. Remove from fire and add cream.

4. To assemble, spread 1/3 of the white sauce in a baking dish.
5. Place ½ of the eggplant slices on it. Sprinkle 2 tbsp cheese on it.
6. Spread ½ of the prepared tomato sauce over the eggplants.
7. Make another layer with the remaining eggplants. Sprinkle a little cheese on them.
8. Top with the remaining tomato sauce.
9. Spread the remaining white sauce also. Sprinkle left over cheese. Bake for 10 minutes at 200°C till cheese melts and turns golden.

Baked Fish with Chutney

Serves 8

½ kg fish fillets
2 tbsp oil

CHUTNEY
½ of a fresh coconut
1 cup chopped coriander leaves, ¼ cup mint (poodina) leaves
4 green chillies, ½" piece ginger, 6 flakes garlic
2 tbsp lime juice
1 tsp salt, 1 tsp sugar

1. Grind all the chutney ingredients to a paste with minimum water.
2. Grease an ovenproof dish. Layer it with half the fish and spread some chutney on the fish. Sprinkle a little oil. Put another layer of fish and chutney and sprinkle oil again. Bake at 180°C/350°F/Gas mark 4 for 40 minutes or till fish is tender.

Note: Rub fish with salt and a little turmeric and keep aside for 1-2 hours to remove the fishy smell. Wash and proceed.

Stuffed Cabbage Rolls

A very unusual baked dish. The sweet and sour sauce makes the cabbage really amazing! Must give it a try.

Serves 6-8   *Picture on page 29*

8 outer large cabbage leaves
2 onions - chopped
1½ cups paneer - crumbled (200 gm)
1½ cups tomato puree
1 tsp vinegar
2 flakes garlic - crushed
4 tbsp oil
1 tsp sugar
1 tsp salt, ½ tsp pepper

1. To break the outer leaves, cut leaves from the stalk end and gently pull from the cut end to get a whole leaf.
2. Boil 6-7 cups of water in a large pan with 2 tsp of salt and 1 tsp sugar. Add cabbage leaves to the boiling water. Cook cabbage in boiling salted water for 3-4 minutes. Drain and cool.
3. Heat 2 tbsp oil. Add onion and cook till golden. Add the paneer and mix well. Add ½ tsp salt & ¼ tsp pepper to taste. Stir for 1 minute and remove from fire.
4. To make the sauce, heat 2 tbsp oil and fry the garlic till it just changes colour. Add the tomato puree, vinegar, sugar, ¾ tsp salt and ½ tsp pepper. Cook for 2 minutes. Remove from fire and check seasonings. Keep aside.
5. Divide the paneer mixture into 8 portions. Place one portion of paneer in the center of a cabbage leaf. Spread it along the width of the leaf and then roll. Cut the hard end of the leaf. Pierce a toothpick on the hard central vein of the leaf.
6. Place the rolls close together in a greased baking dish.
7. Pour the sauce over.
8. Cover and bake in a preheated oven at 180°C/350°F/Gas mark 4 for 25-30 minutes.

Cauliflower Souffle

The souffle should be served straight from the oven, so put it in the oven about 40-50 minutes before the food is going to be served.

Serves 6

1 cauliflower - broken into florets
4 tbsp butter - softened
½ cup flour (maida)
2 cups milk
½ cup grated cheese
2 eggs - separated
4 tbsp chopped coriander or parsley
½ tsp grated nutmeg (jaiphal)
1¼ tsp salt and ½ tsp pepper
½ tsp red chilli flakes

1. Boil 4 cups water with 1 tsp salt. Add cauliflower florets. Boil for 3-4 minutes. Drain and cool. Blend for a few seconds only in a liquidizer to a rough puree.
2. Melt butter, add flour. Stir on low heat for 1 minute. Remove from the heat and add milk. Mix well. Return to fire.
3. Add salt, pepper and nutmeg. Cook till the sauce thickens.
4. Add the grated cheese, cauliflower puree, 2 tbsp of chopped coriander or parsley and egg yolks.
5. Add a pinch of salt to the egg whites and beat till stiff.
6. Fold the egg whites into the mixture.
7. Butter a souffle dish, pour the mixture in it. Sprinkle chopped coriander and freshly crushed black peppercorns or red chilli flakes. Bake at 190C°/375°F/Gas mark 5 for 40-50 minutes.
8. Serve immediately.

Mushroom Pie

Cheesy mushrooms topped with golden mashed potatoes.

Serves 6-8

2 cups potatoes - boiled and grated (4 potatoes)
200 gm mushrooms - chopped
2 tbsp butter - softened
2 eggs
1 large onion - chopped
½ cup grated cheese (50 gm)
3 tbsp dried bread crumbs
1 tsp salt, ½ tsp pepper

TOPPING
2-3 tbsp grated cheese
1 tbsp butter
½ tsp freshly crushed peppercorns (saboot kali mirch)

1. Boil and grate the potatoes.
2. Add ½ tsp salt, ¼ tsp pepper and 1 tbsp butter. Mix.
3. Saute the chopped mushrooms in 1 tbsp butter for 2-3 minutes. Keep aside.
4. Beat eggs in a bowl. Add chopped onion, cheese and bread crumbs to the beaten eggs.
5. Mix it with the mushrooms and add ½ tsp salt and ¼ tsp pepper.
6. Spread the mixture evenly in a buttered medium oven proof glass dish.
7. Spread the mashed potatoes over the mushrooms, sprinkle with some cheese and dot with butter. Sprinkle crushed peppercorns.
8. Bake in a preheated oven at 190C°/375°F/Gas mark 4 for 40-45 minutes until the top is brown. Serve hot.

Moussaka

A classic Greek dish of aubergines and minced lamb.

Serves 6-8

**2 aubergines (brinjals), thin long variety, 2 potatoes - boiled and sliced
2 tomatoes - blanched and chopped
500 gm lamb mince (keema)
2 large onions - finely chopped, 4-6 flakes garlic - crushed & chopped finely
2 tbsp tomato puree, ¼ tsp pepper, 1 tsp salt or to taste
4-5 tbsp olive oil or any cooking oil, ½ tsp red chilli flakes, ½ tsp oregano**

**CHEESE SAUCE
2 tbsp butter - softened, 3 tbsp plain flour (maida)
1¼ cups (300 ml) milk , 1 egg, 1 cube cheese - grated (4 tbsp)
salt to taste, ½ tsp mustard paste**

1. Thinly slice the aubergines (baingan) and arrange them in a large plate. Sprinkle salt on both sides. Let the aubergines stand for ½ hour to drain out juices. Rinse the aubergine slices in cold water and pat dry.
2. Heat 1 cup oil in a kadhai or frying pan and fry the aubergine and potato slices until brown. Drain on paper napkins or absorbent paper. Keep aside.
3. Put tomatoes in boiling water for 2 min. Drain. Peel the outer skin. Chop finely.
4. Heat 4-5 tbsp of olive oil in a pressure cooker, add the chopped onion and stir.
5. Add the garlic and cook till the onions turn pink.
6. Add the tomatoes stir fry till the juices evaporate and tomatoes turn dry.
7. Add the mince and cook on high flame until brown and dry.
8. Add tomato puree, chilli flakes, oregano, salt and pepper. Add ½ to ¾ cup of water and pressure cook to give one whistle, reduce the flame and simmer for 1-2 minutes. Remove from flame. Cool.
9. Check for tenderness and cook till almost dry. Dry the excess liquid but do not make it too dry. Adjust the seasoning according to taste. Keep aside.
10. To prepare the cheese sauce, heat butter in a heavy bottomed pan, add flour, stir gently on low flame for 1 minute till it slightly changes colour. Remove from heat. Add the milk and mix well. Return to heat and cook till the sauce becomes thick. Add salt, pepper, mustard and cheese. Remove from heat and cool slightly.
11. Add the beaten egg to the cooled white sauce. Keep aside.
12. To assemble, spoon half of the meat mixture in a shallow ovenproof dish. Top with half the aubergine and potato slices. Repeat with the remaining meat and vegetable slices. Then pour the cheese sauce. Cook in a preheated oven at 200°C for 25-30 minutes or until bubbling hot and browned. Serve with garlic bread.

Chicken Vegetable Potato Pie

An interesting chicken pie flavoured with vegetable soup and topped with mashed potatoes.

Serves 2-3

250 gm boneless chicken pieces - cut into 1 " pieces
4 tbsp butter - softened
½ packet ready made vegetable soup
2 cups boiled and grated potatoes (4)
1 tsp salt, ½ tsp pepper
½ cup grated cheese (50 gm)
2 tbsp chopped parsley or coriander
¼ tsp peppercorns - crushed

1. In a kadhai, melt 1 tbsp of butter, add the chicken pieces and fry on medium heat till golden brown. Add ¼ tsp salt and ¼ tsp pepper. Remove chicken from the kadhai and keep aside.
2. Dissolve ½ packet of soup in ¼ cup water. Boil 1 cup of water. Add the dissolved soup to boiling water and cook stirring continuously for about 5 minutes till the soup turns thick. Add ¼ tsp salt and ¼ tsp pepper or to taste.
3. Place the chicken pieces in a greased glass baking dish and pour the soup.
4. To the mashed potatoes add 3 tbsp butter, ¼ tsp salt and ¼ tsp pepper. Mix well.
5. Lay the potato mixture over the chicken. Mark it with a fork.
6. Sprinkle cheese on it.
7. Sprinkle some chopped coriander or parsley.
8. Sprinkle some crushed peppercorns.
9. Bake in a preheated oven at 185°C/375°F/Gas mark 5 for 20 minutes or till potatoes turn golden.

French Style Eggs

in Mushroom Sauce

Whole eggs are baked on a bed of mushrooms.

Serves 4

4 eggs
2 large tomatoes - blanched, peeled and chopped
2 cups chopped mushrooms
2 tbsp olive oil, or any cooking oil
1 onion - chopped
2 flakes garlic - crushed
1 tbsp chopped green coriander
1 tsp chopped green chilli
1 tsp salt, ½ tsp pepper, or to taste

1. Blanch the tomatoes in boiling water for 3-4 minutes. Peel and chop finely.
2. Chop the mushrooms into small pieces.
3. Heat the olive oil. Add onions and garlic and stir fry till light brown.
4. Add mushrooms and stir fry for 5 minutes.
5. Add tomatoes, coriander leaves, green chilli, salt and pepper. Cook for another 5 minutes till slightly thick. Pour the mixture in a greased glass baking dish.
6. Make four hollows in the mushroom mixture in the dish and break in the eggs taking care not to break the yolks.
7. Bake in a preheated oven at 180°C/350°F/Gas mark 4 for 8-10 minutes or until the egg white is set. Serve with toasts.

Mutton Hot Pot

Picture on cover   *Serves 6-8*

½ kg boneless mutton - cut into 1" pieces
4 large onions - cut into rings
2-3 thin long brinjals - sliced
2 large potatoes - peeled and cut into thin slices
½ tsp ground cinnamon (dalchini)
1 magie chicken stock cube - mixed with ½ cup water
1 cup ready made tomato puree
1 tsp salt, ½ tsp pepper
6 tbsp oil

1. Fry the boneless mutton pieces in 6 tbsp oil in a pressure cooker for 5 minutes.
2. Add onions and stir fry till golden.
3. Add 1 cup of water, 1 tsp salt, ¼ tsp pepper, ¼ tsp cinnamon powder and pressure cook for 15 minutes or till the mutton is tender.
4. Take a glass oven proof dish.
5. Mix sliced brinjals and the remaining sliced onions and season with ½ tsp salt, ¼ tsp pepper and ½ tsp cinnamon.
6. With half of the brinjal mixture, put a layer of it in the prepared baking dish.
7. Put the cooked mutton on top.
8. Cover again with the remaining onions and brinjals.
9. Mix the tomato puree to the stock cube dissolved in ½ cup of water and pour this over the brinjals.
10. Cut the potatoes into thin slices. Sprinkle some salt, pepper and 1 tbsp oil on them and mix well. Spread them on top. Brush them with oil.
11. Cover with foil and bake in a preheated oven at 180°C/350°F/Gas mark 4 for 1½ hours. Serve hot.

Fish Flan

A melt in your mouth dish with the simplest ingredients.

Picture on facing page   *Serves 6-8*

½ kg (5) boiled potatoes
250 gm white fish fillet
1 big onion - chopped
1 egg - separated
5 tbsp butter - softened
2 tbsp flour (maida)
2 bay leaves (tej patta)
1 tsp salt, ½ tsp pepper
2 tbsp chopped parsley or coriander

1. Spread aluminium foil on the back of a baking tray. Grease it well with butter or oil.
2. Mash the potatoes and add 3 tbsp butter, egg yolk, ½ tsp salt and ¼ tsp pepper.
3. On the aluminium sheet, shape the potatoes into a flat round of about 7" and build the edge up to about 1" height.
4. Bake at 180°C/350°F/Gas mark 4 for about 15 minutes.
5. Cook the fish with 1¼ cups water, ½ onion, bay leaf and ½ tsp salt. Keep fish and the liquid aside. Discard the bay leaf.
6. Melt the remaining butter, add onion and saute for a few seconds. Add the flour, gently cook for a few minutes, stirring all the time.
7. Remove from the heat add ¾ cup liquid from the boiled fish. Stir well and cook for a few minutes longer till it turns a little thick.
8. Flake the fish coarsely and add the sauce to it. Add parsley or coriander and mix. Check seasonings.
9. Whisk the egg white until stiff with a pinch of salt and fold into the fish mixture.
10. Pour fish mixture into the potato case.
11. Bake at 180°C/350°F/Gas mark 4 for 20 minutes until the top is golden brown.

Note: To remove the smell of the fish, marinate the fish with some salt and turmeric powder.

Stuffed Cabbage Rolls : Recipe on page 21, Fish Flan ➤

Chicken Baked with Macaroni

A creamy chicken baked with macaroni & topped with toasted almonds.

Serves 4-5

250-300 gm boneless chicken - cut into 1" pieces
50 gm macaroni (½ cup)
1 tbsp butter
1 small capsicum - deseeded and chopped
1 small firm tomato - deseeded and chopped

SAUCE
1 small onion - chopped
2 tbsp butter, 2½ tbsp flour (maida)
1 cup milk
4 tbsp tomato puree, 1 tbsp tomato sauce
salt and pepper to taste
2 tbsp chopped parsley or coriander

GARNISH
3-4 almonds - cut into thin long pieces
some grated cheese

1. Heat 1 tbsp butter in a pressure cooker. Add the chicken pieces and stir fry for 2-3 minutes. Add 1½ cups water and pressure cook to give 2 whistles. Reduce heat and simmer for 2-3 minutes. Remove from heat. Cool. Strain and reserve the stock for sauce and keep the chicken pieces aside.

2. Boil 2 cups of water. Add macaroni and boil for 7-8 minutes till tender. Drain and refresh under cold water. Strain and keep aside in the strainer for all the water to drain out.

3. To prepare the sauce, heat butter in a pan and add onions. Stir till they turn soft and slightly change colour. Add the flour and stir till light brown. Mix stock and milk to get 2½ cups. Lower heat and add the stock-milk mixture. Stir till smooth and creamy. Remove from heat. Add tomato puree, tomato sauce, salt, pepper and chopped parsley or coriander.

4. Add macaroni, chicken, capsicum and tomato. Stir well and check the seasoning, adjust according to taste.

5. Pour the mixture in a baking dish. Top with grated cheese and almonds. Bake in a moderate oven at 180°C for 15 minutes. Serve hot with buttered toasts cut into triangles.

Lasange with Minced Mutton

An Italian favourite!

Serves 8
Picture on page 1

½ kg minced mutton (keema)
1 tsp salt, ½ tsp pepper
2 cups ready made tomato puree
8 lasagne sheets, ready made
4 tbsp oil
1 cup grated cheese, preferably mozzarella

SAUCE
2¼ cups milk
3 tbsp butter - softened, 4 tbsp flour (maida)
½ cup grated cheese
½ tsp salt, ¼ tsp freshly ground pepper

1. Cook the mince in 4 tbsp oil in a pressure cooker for 5 minutes and add salt and pepper.
2. Add tomato puree and ½ cup of water. Pressure cook for 10 minutes till mince is tender and the gravy turns thick.
3. In a shallow pan or a kadhai boil water with some salt, slip one sheet at a time to prevent them from sticking together. When one is half done, slip the second one. Do not boil too many sheets at a time.
4. Simmer gently for about 5 minutes or until they are tender.
5. Remove, run cold water over them. Keep them separately covered with a damp cloth.
6. To make the sauce melt butter, add the flour and stir for 1 minute on low heat. Add the milk, stirring continuously. Stir until the sauce comes to a boil. Remove from fire.
7. Add the grated cheese and season with salt and pepper.
8. To assemble the lasagne, grease a rectangle or square baking dish with some butter or oil. Spread 2-3 tbsp sauce at the bottom of the dish. Put a layer of cooked lasagne sheet in the dish.
9. Spread 2 heaped tbsp of mince mixture on the lasagne sheet.
10. Pour just a little sauce (about 2 tbsp) over the mince. Sprinkle some cheese.
11. Continue the layers in this way until all the mixture is used, ending with a thick layer of sauce.
12. Sprinkle ½ cup grated cheese evenly over the surface.
13. Cover loosely with aluminium foil and bake in a hot oven at 180°C/350°F/Gas mark 6 for 25 minutes. Uncover and bake for another 10 minutes. Serve hot.

Bread & Cheese Bake

A good dish when you have nothing substantial in the house! Just bread & cheese is enough.

Serves 6-8

6 bread slices
1½ cups grated cheese (150 gm)
3 tbsp butter - softened
1½ cups milk
2 tbsp flour (maida)
½ tsp mustard powder or paste
½ tsp salt and ½ tsp freshly ground pepper

1. Heat 2 tbsp of butter. Add the flour and stir for a minute on low heat. Add milk stirring continuously. Cook till thick.
2. Season with salt, pepper and mustard. Keep white sauce aside.
3. Butter the bread slices nicely and crumble it with your hands.
4. Grease an oven proof dish and spread a layer using ½ of the fresh bread crumbs.
5. Sprinkle 1/3 of the cheese on the bread.
6. Repeat the bread layer using all the left over bread.
7. Sprinkle half the cheese.
8. Pour the cheese sauce to cover nicely. Sprinkle the remaining cheese and top with 4-5 freshly crushed peppercorns.
9. Bake in a preheated oven at 180°C/350°F/Gas mark 4 for 30 minutes.

Tomato & Mozzarella Bake

Cheese and tomato slices over garlic flavoured bread.

Serves 6

½ kg tomatoes (5-6)
100-150 gm mozzarella cheese
4-6 bread slices - crust removed
2 onions - finely chopped, 2 flakes garlic - finely chopped
6 tbsp oil
1 tsp salt, ½ tsp pepper, ½ tsp oregano

1. Cut tomatoes into ¼" thick slices and cheese also into slices of similar size and thickness.
2. Heat 2 tbsp oil. Add onions, garlic and ¼ tsp salt. Cook till onions turn soft.
3. Cover the base of a greased baking dish with bread slices, trimming them to fit. Pour 2 tbsp oil on the bread.
4. Sprinkle the onion and garlic mixture, keeping a little for the top.
5. Arrange tomato and cheese slices alternately on top of bread. Sprinkle them with salt, pepper and oregano.
6. Spoon the rest of the oil (2 tbsp) and onion and garlic mixture on the cheese - tomato layer. Bake in a preheated oven 220°C/425°F/Gas mark 7 for 30 minutes.

Nest Eggs

Whole eggs cooked in tomato cases which are embedded in tomato sauce.

Serves 4

4 large tomatoes
4 large eggs
½ cup grated cheese
1 flake garlic - crushed
¾ tsp salt, ½ tsp pepper

1. Slice the top of the tomatoes, carefully remove the pulp and reserve the pulp.
2. Mix the garlic with the tomato pulp. Add salt and pepper and cook till it thickens.
3. Break the eggs one by one in the tomatoes carefully so as not to break the yolks.
4. Place the tomatoes in a baking dish . Pour the pulp around the tomatoes.
5. Sprinkle grated cheese on top.
6. Bake it for 8-10 minutes or till the yolk is cooked. Serve immediately.

Baked Lemon Chicken

Serves 6

½ kg boneless chicken pieces
2 tbsp lemon juice
2 bay leaves (tej patta)
6 baby onions (very small) - peeled or 2 small onions - each cut into 4 pieces
½ cup carrot - diced
½ cup mushroom - sliced (100 gm)
4 tbsp butter - softened
4-5 almonds - blanched and split into 2 halves

MIX TOGETHER
4 tbsp cream
1 egg
½ tsp salt, ½ tsp pepper

1. Cook chicken pieces with lemon juice, bay leaves, ½ tsp salt, ¼ tsp pepper and 1 cup water in a pressure cooker till tender, for about 5 minutes.
2. When tender remove the chicken from the liquid. Keep stock aside.
3. Fry mushrooms, diced carrots and small onions in butter for 5 minutes. Add ¼ tsp salt and ¼ tsp pepper.
4. Beat the egg and cream together and gradually add 1 cup of boiling stock. Keep on low heat and cook stirring continuously until smooth and coats the spoon. Add ½ tsp salt and ¼ tsp pepper. Remove sauce from fire.
5. In a greased shallow glass dish, arrange the chicken pieces and then the sauteed vegetables on the chicken.
6. Top with blanched (skinned) almonds.
7. Pour the sauce and bake for 15 minutes at 180°C/350°F/Gas mark 4.
8. Serve with bread.

Note: Cook the egg and cream sauce in a heavy bottomed kadhai, on very low heat stirring continuously, to avoid the egg from curdling.

Nutty Baked Cabbage

The nuts add a wonderful nutty flavour and crunch to the cabbage. A very simple dish to prepare when you are pressed for time.

Serves 4

3 cups cabbage - shredded
1 tsp ginger paste
1 tsp garlic paste
¾ cup cream
½ cup nuts (walnuts, cashewnuts and peanuts) - chopped
1 tsp sugar
½ salt
¼ tsp black pepper
4 tbsp bread crumbs
1/3 cup grated cheese

1. Heat 3 tbsp oil in a frying pan with ginger and garlic. Add cabbage and toss, cover the pan and cook on low heat for 5 minutes, tossing once or twice in between. Add ½ tsp salt. Mix well. Remove from fire.
2. Combine cream with sugar, ½ tsp salt, ¼ tsp pepper and nuts in a bowl.
3. Pour cream mixture over the cabbage.
4. Pour into a baking dish and sprinkle bread curmbs. Bake in a moderate oven 160°C/325°F/Gas mark 3 for 30 minutes.
5. Sprinkle cheese and place under a grill till cheese melts.

Pasta with Mushrooms
& Tomatoes

A very quick, yet delightful recipe.

Serves 6

1½ cups pasta (macaroni, penne or any other type)
2 cups mushrooms - chopped (200 gm)
1 onion - chopped
4 large tomatoes - blanched, peeled and cut into round slices
3 tbsp oil
¾ cup grated cheese, preferably mozzarella cheese
½ cup cream (Vijaya or fresh)
1 tsp salt, ¼ tsp pepper

1. Boil pasta with 1 tsp of oil and ½ tsp salt for 10 minutes or until just tender. Drain and put in cold water. Strain and keep aside.
2. Heat the oil and fry the chopped onion until soft.
3. Add mushrooms, ½ tsp salt and pepper and fry for 5 minutes.
4. Put the tomatoes in boiling water for 2 minutes. Remove from water. Peel the skin and cut them into round slices.
5. In a large greased dish put a layer of pasta, top with onion and mushrooms. Cover with sliced tomatoes.
6. Lastly sprinkle half the cheese.
7. Mix cream with ¼ tsp salt and ¼ tsp pepper. Pour the cream over the tomatoes. Spread the cream all over with the back of a spoon.
8. Top with the remaining grated cheese.
9. Bake in a preheated oven at 200°C/400°F/Gas mark 6 for 15-20 minutes.

Baked Vegetables in Spinach Sauce

A tasty and nourishing baked dish.

Serves 6

3 cups - diced mixed vegetables (french beans, carrots, green peas, cauliflower and potatoes)
1 onion - sliced finely
1 tbsp butter - softened
1 tsp red chilli powder, ½ tsp salt

WHITE SAUCE
2 tbsp flour (maida)
2 tbsp butter - softened
1 cup milk
1¼ tsp salt, ½ tsp pepper

OTHER INGREDIENTS
2 cups chopped spinach
1 cup cream
6 tbsp grated cheese

1. Steam or microwave the vegetables. To microwave the vegetables, put them in a bowl. Add ½ cup water and ½ tsp salt. Mix well and micro high covered for about 4 minutes till crisp-tender. Strain and keep aside.
2. Heat 1 tbsp butter and fry the onions till soft.
3. Add mixed vegetables and saute for a minute.
4. Add chilli powder and ½ tsp salt. Keep aside.
5. To make the white sauce, heat 2 tbsp butter. Add 2 tbsp flour and stir till flour turns light brown. Remove from fire and add milk. Add ½ tsp salt and ¼ tsp pepper. Cook till thick. Keep aside.
6. Cook the spinach separately till dry.
7. When cool, blend in a liquidizer to a puree.
8. Beat the cream lightly, add the white sauce and spinach puree to it. Add ¼ tsp salt and ¼ tsp pepper.
9. Mix the vegetables with sauce. Mix 3 tbsp grated cheese. Check the salt and pepper.
10. Pour in a greased baking dish and sprinkle the rest of cheese on the top.
11. Bake in a preheated oven at 200°C/400°F for 15-20 minutes. Serve hot.

Lentil Shepherd's Pie

Picture on facing page   Serves 8

PRESSURE COOK TOGETHER
1 cup brown lentils (saboot masoor)
1 tbsp oil, 1 tsp salt, 1 " piece ginger - chopped
2½ cups water

OTHER INGREDIENTS FOR THE FILLING
2 tbsp olive oil or any cooking oil
a pinch asafoetida powder (hing)
½ tsp freshly ground black pepper
1 large carrot - cut into tiny pieces (1 cup)
½ cup boiled peas
100 gm cottage cheese (paneer) - crumbled
½ tsp soya sauce

POTATO TOPPING
5 potatoes - boiled, peeled, grated and mashed till smooth
2-3 tbsp butter - softened, ¼ cup hot milk
1¼ tsp salt, ½ tsp pepper, 2 tbsp cream or well beaten malai
3 tbsp chopped fresh parsley or coriander, juice of ½ lemon, or to taste

1. Pressure cook lentils with 1 tbsp oil, chopped ginger, salt and 2½ cups water to give 1 whistle. Simmer on low heat for 10-12 minutes. Remove from fire and keep aside. If there is any water, dry on fire.

2. Mash grated potatoes until smooth. Add butter, milk, salt, pepper, cream, coriander or parsley and lemon juice to the mashed potatoes. Mix well. Keep aside.

3. To prepare the filling, heat oil in a small, heavy pan or kadhai. Add the asafoetida and pepper and saute for 3-4 seconds. Add the carrots and stir for 1 minute. Cover and cook on low heat for 2-3 minutes till soft. Add peas. Add ¼ tsp salt. Remove from heat. Keep aside.

4. Crumble the cottage cheese in a bowl and add ½ tsp salt and soya sauce. Mix.

5. Combine cottage cheese, lentils and the cooked carrots and peas.

6. Spread this pie filling evenly at the bottom of a greased oven-proof dish.

7. Cover the mixture with the potatoes, level the potatoes with a knife. Ripple or score the potato mixture with a fork in a decorative design, by making lines on the potato topping as shown in the picture.

8. Preheat oven to 200°C. Bake for 25-30 minutes till the potato topping turns golden. Serve hot.

Florets in Broccoli Sauce : Recipe on page 52, Lentil Shepherd's Pie ➤

Crisp Cheesy Potato Bake

You will never imagine how tasty potatoes can be!

Serves 6

4 big (½ kg) potatoes - peeled and cut into very thin slices
4-5 tbsp melted butter
1 cup grated cheese (100 gm)
1 cup cream
1 tsp salt and ½ tsp pepper

1. Wash the potatoes. Peel and slice them very thinly.
2. Grease a glass oven proof dish and put a layer with some slices of potatoes, sprinkle cheese on them and finally pour some melted butter.
3. Repeat layers of potato slices, cheese and butter till all the potatoes are used up.
4. Mix1 tsp salt and ½ tsp pepper in 1 cup cream.
5. Pour the cream on the potatoes.
6. Sprinkle cheese.
7. Crush 5-6 peppercorns and sprinkle on the cheese.
8. Cover with aluminium foil and bake in a preheated oven at 180°C/350°F/Gas mark 4 for about 60 minutes till the potatoes are tender and crisp. Check the potatoes before removing the dish from the oven. Serve.

Spinach Pie

Whole spinach leaves with potatoes - baked with eggs till firm such that it can be cut into wedges like a pie.

Serves 6

6 medium (½ kg) potatoes - boiled
1 small bundle (½ kg) spinach
½ cup grated cheese
2 tsp oil
2 eggs
½ cup cream
a pinch of nutmeg (jaiphal)
¾ tsp salt and ¼ tsp pepper, or to taste

1. Peel and cut the potatoes into thin round slices.
2. Break leaves of spinach, discarding the stalks. Wash leaves nicely. Boil 5-6 cups water with 1 tsp sugar and 2 tsp salt. Add the spinach leaves in boiling water. Boil for 30 seconds. Drain and pour iced water on it to refresh it. Strain and squeeze gently. Keep aside.
3. Beat the eggs in a bowl. Add the cream, nutmeg, salt and pepper. Beat till well mixed.
4. Grease a glass pie dish.
5. Arrange a layer of sliced potatoes using half of the potatoes. Sprinkle a pinch of salt and pepper.
6. Spread half of the spinach leaves.
7. Pour half of the egg mixture and sprinkle some cheese. Repeat the four layers again.
8. Bake in a preheated oven at 180°C/300°F/Gas mark 3 for 30 minutes or until firm and the potatoes are crisp golden.
9. To serve, cut the pie in 8 wedges.

Shahi Gobi

A baked dish for the typical Indian palate.

Serves 6

1 medium size cauliflower
1 tsp garlic paste, 1 tsp ginger paste
½ tsp green chilli paste
1 tbsp lemon juice
½ tsp garam masala, ½ tsp salt to taste

MASALA
3 large tomatoes
5 tbsp oil
1 tsp garlic paste
1 tsp ginger paste
1 tsp cumin (jeera) powder
1 tsp coriander (dhania) powder
¼ cup curd - beat till smooth
3 onions - chopped
1½ tsp salt, ½ tsp pepper
2 tbsp coriander leaves

1. Mix the ginger, garlic and green chilli paste with lemon juice.
2. Add garam masala and ½ tsp salt.
3. Insert the paste inside the florets of the cauliflower, some from the top and inserting some paste from below also.
4. Put the cauliflower in a metal bowl with the stem downwards.
5. Put the metal bowl in a large pressure cooker containing 1½ cups water. Steam for 5 minutes. Check to see that the stalks are soft and the cauliflower cooked.
6. Blanch the tomatoes, remove the skin and grind them in a mixer to a puree.
7. Heat oil and fry the onions till golden. Add ginger & garlic paste. Mix well.
8. Add curd and ½ tsp salt. Mix well.
9. Add the tomato puree. Boil. Simmer for 7-8 minutes. Keep masala paste aside.
10. Place the cauliflower, leaving behind the water, very carefully in an oven proof dish and cover it with half the masala paste.
11. Bake in a preheated oven at 180°C/350°F/Gas mark 4 for 15 minutes or till masala is brown.
12. Remove from the oven and pour the remaining masala on all the sides of the cauliflower. Bake for another 10 minutes. Sprinkle coriander leaves and serve.

Sweet Corn Pie

Check that the corn kernels are really sweet to get a sweet & salty pie.

Serves 6

niblets of 1 large sweet corn tin (1 cup), see note
2 cups milk
2 tbsp butter - softened
2 tbsp flour (maida)
½ cup grated cheese
½ tsp salt, ¼ tsp pepper
3 tbsp chopped coriander, preferably the stalks

1. Heat the butter and cook the flour on low heat for 1 minute.
2. Add the milk, stirring continuously. Add ½ tsp salt, ¼ tsp pepper and stir till it comes to a boil.
3. When the sauce is thick, add the cheese and mix well.
4. Mix in the corn and coriander. Remove from fire.
5. Pour the mixture in a greased oven proof dish.
6. Bake in a preheated oven at 180°C/350°F/Gas mark 4 for 25-30 minutes or until golden brown.

Note: If using fresh or frozen corn, boil it in 3 cups water with a pinch of haldi, 1 tsp salt and 1 tbsp sugar added to the water to get sweet corn niblets.

Bread Stuffed Green Peppers

An unusual stuffing of bread in capsicums.

Serves 4

4 green peppers or capsicums
6 slices white bread
4 tbsp milk
2 tbsp coriander - chopped
1 onion - chopped
2 tbsp tomato sauce
½ cup cheese spread or cream cheese
¾ tsp salt, ¼ tsp pepper, or to taste

1. Cut off the top of the peppers and scoop out the seeds and core. If you want to make them decorative, cut the top in a zig-zag manner (VVV) with the help of a kitchen scissors.
2. Boil them in salted hot water for 2-3 minutes.
3. Soften the bread with milk. Crumble the bread.
4. Add the tomato sauce, coriander leaves, chopped onion and the cheese to the bread. Season with ¾ tsp salt and ¼ tsp pepper and mix well.
5. Fill the peppers with this mixture and replace the caps. Brush with oil or melted butter on the outside of the capsicum.
6. Arrange the stuffed peppers in a baking tin and bake in a preheated oven at 180°/350°F/Gas mark 4 for 30-35 minutes until soft.

Mushrooms & Macaroni
in Spinach Sesame Sauce

Serves 4-5   *Picture on page 19*

1 cup uncooked macaroni
100 gm mushrooms - sliced
50 gm baby corns - sliced (optional)
2 tbsp butter - softened
1 tsp oregano
½ salt, ¼ tsp pepper, or to taste
½ capsicum - cut into ½" squares

SAUCE
½ tsp sesame seeds (til)
¾ cup very finely chopped spinach
2½ tbsp butter
2½ tbsp flour (maida)
2 cups milk
½ tsp salt, ¼ tsp freshly ground saboot kali mirch (peppercorns)

TOPPING
1 tbsp bread crumbs
½ tsp sesame seeds (til) or khus khus (poppy seeds)
a few tomato slices

1. Boil macaroni in salted water till done. Strain and refresh in cold water.
2. Heat 2 tbsp butter in a large non-stick pan. Add mushrooms. Stir fry till golden.
3. Add baby corns and boiled macaroni.
4. Sprinkle salt, pepper and oregano. Mix well. Remove from fire.
5. Add capsicum. Transfer to a greased baking dish.
6. For sauce, heat butter. Add sesame seeds. Wit till golden.
7. Add spinach and cook till dry.
8. Add flour. Stir on low heat for 1 minute. Add milk, stirring continuously, till sauce turns thick. Add salt and pepper. Cook for 2-3 minutes on low heat.
9. Pour the spinach sauce over the macaroni in the dish.
10. Arrange a few tomato slices. Top with bread crumbs and sesame seeds.
11. Bake at 180°C for 20 minutes till golden. Serve hot.

Baked Vegetable Rosti

Vegetables topped with a potato pancake.

Serves 6

1 eggplant (round one) - cut into ½" cubes
2 zucchinis or tori - ½"cubes
1 green pepper (capsicum) - cut into ¼" pieces
3 tbsp oil
¼ tsp asafoetida (hing)
¼ tsp pepper - freshly ground, salt to taste
2 tomatoes - blanched, peeled & cut into eights
1 tbsp parsley or coriander - chopped

ROSTI (POTATO PANCAKE)
3 potatoes - peeled, steamed or microwaved, till barely cooked and cooled
2 tsp cornflour
1 tbsp butter, 1 tbsp olive oil or any other cooking oil
¼ tsp pepper, ½ tsp salt, or to taste

SAUCE
1 tbsp butter - softened, ¼ cup tomato puree
1 tsp cornflour mixed with ¼ cup water, salt and pepper to taste

1. Place the eggplants in a colander. Sprinkle salt and keep aside for 15 minutes. Rinse thoroughly. Drain and pat the eggplants with a clean kitchen towel till dry.
2. Heat oil. Add hing and fry for a few seconds.
3. Add eggplant and saute for 3-4 minutes till light brown.
4. Add zucchini, ¼ tsp salt and black pepper. Cover and cook on low heat for 5-7 minutes till zucchini is done. Add capsicum.
5. Add tomatoes and cook until they warm through.
6. Add coriander or parsley. Mix. Keep aside.
7. To prepare the sauce, heat butter. Add all ingredients of the sauce and cook till thick. Remove from fire and keep aside.
8. To prepare the rosti, grate cold potatoes coarsely. Mix in the cornflour lightly. Keep aside.
9. Melt butter and oil together in a large, heavy pan over medium heat.
10. Add grated potatoes and spread out into a large pancake, (size of dish) taking care not to press it down too much. Sprinkle salt and pepper on the pancake.
11. Cover and cook till the underside of the pancake starts to brown. Shake pan once or twice in between.

12. Over turn only when the underside is well browned on to a plate. Return to the pan to cook the other side. Sprinkle salt and pepper on the other side too. Cook till ready. Remove from fire and let it be in the pan.
13. To assemble, pour ½ of the sauce at the bottom of a round dish, which is about the size of the pancake. Spread vegetables on the sauce. Pour the left over sauce on the vegetables. Gently slide the pancake from the pan on to the vegetables. Grate cheese and dot with butter. Sprinkle chopped coriander.
14. Bake for 15 minutes till cheese turns golden.

Greens Baked with Corn

Serves 6

3 cups finely chopped mixed greens (spinach, cabbage, broccoli)
1 cup grated paneer, ½ tsp red chilli flakes
½ cup boiled or tinned corn kernels
2 tbsp butter or oil
4-5 flakes garlic - crushed, 1 onion - thinly sliced
8-10 peppercorns - crushed coarsely
1 tomato cut into slices and some mint leaves - to garnish
2 tbsp mozzarella cheese - grated

SAUCE
2 tbsp butter - softened, 2 tbsp plain flour (maida)
1½ cups milk
salt to pepper to taste, 2 tbsp mozzarella cheese - grated

1. Boil 5-6 cups water with 2 tsp salt and 2 tsp sugar. Add the greens to boiling water. As soon as the boil returns, remove from fire and strain. Refresh with cold water.
2. Heat 2 tbsp butter or oil. Saute garlic and sliced onion till onion turns transparent. Add crushed peppercorns and ½ tsp salt. Squeeze greens gently and add to the onions. Cook till dry for 2 minutes. Remove from fire.
3. To prepare the sauce, heat butter. Add flour. Cook for 1 minute. Add milk, stirring continuously. Stir till a little thick. Add salt and pepper to taste. Add 2 tbsp cheese. Keep aside.
4. In a dish arrange the greens to form 1½-2" thick layer. Sprinkle grated paneer.
5. Spread cooked corn (not too much) on it. Sprinkle some salt and red chilli flakes on it. Pour the prepared sauce. Sprinkle grated cheese.
6. Arrange slices of tomatoes on it. Bake at 230°C for 8-10 minutes or till cheese melts. Garnish with mint leaves.

Vegetable Au Gratin

The All time favourite! A little tomato sauce added to the sauce makes it more delicious.

Picture on facing page   Serves 6

WHITE SAUCE
4 tbsp butter softened, 4 tbsp flour (maida)
2½ cups milk
1½ tsp salt, or to taste
½ tsp saboot kali mirch (peppercorns) - crushed to a powder
1 tbsp tomato ketchup, 2 tbsp grated cheese, (mozzarella or pizza cheese)

VEGETABLES
10-15 french beans - cut diagonally into small pieces
2 carrots - cut into small cubes
½ cup shelled peas
½ small cauliflower - cut into small florets
1 medium potato - cut into small cubes
½ small (250 gms) ghiya (bottle gourd) - cut into small cubes

OTHER INGREDIENTS
½ cup grated cheese, (mozzarella or pizza cheese)

1. Wash vegetables & pressure cook with 1 tsp salt with ¼ cup water, till the hissing sound starts. Remove from fire before the whistle. You may also microwave the vegetables. To microwave, wash chopped vegetables and micro high covered for 4-5 minutes with ¼ cup water till crisp tender. Keep aside.
2. To prepare the sauce, heat butter in a clean heavy bottomed pan, on low flame.
3. When butter melts, add the flour and mix stirring continuously on low flame for 1 minute. Do not let the colour change.
4. Remove from fire and add milk. Mix well. Return to fire and stir continuously till the sauce becomes thick.
5. Add salt, pepper and tomato ketchup to it.
6. Mix steamed vegetables and also the water in it with the sauce. Add salt if required. Cook till the water gets evaporated (for about 2 minutes) and the sauce coats the vegetables well.
7. Remove from fire and mix in the cheese.
8. Transfer to a shallow borosil dish. Sprinkle grated cheese. Bake in a hot oven at 200°C, till golden brown for about 25 minutes. Remove from the oven and serve hot.

Fresh Fruit Tarts : Recipe on page 105, Vegetable Au Gratin ➤

Shredded Spinach Bake

Spinach shreds with some mushrooms baked in cheese sauce.

Serves 8

3 cups shredded (cut into thin ribbons) spinach
¾ cup mushrooms - sliced
2 tbsp butter - softened
2 onions - chopped
2 flakes garlic - chopped
salt and pepper

CHEESE SAUCE
1½ cups milk
3 tbsp flour (maida)
½ cup grated cheese
¾ tsp salt, ¼ tsp pepper
1½ tbsp butter - softened

1. Boil ½ cup water with ½ tsp sugar and 1 tsp salt. Add spinach. Mix well. Keep on fire for 2 minutes. Remove from fire and strain. Squeeze the spinach in the strainer to drain out the water. Keep aside.
2. Heat 2 tbsp butter add garlic and onion. Cook till onion turn soft.
3. Add ½ tsp salt. Add spinach and cook till dry.
4. Add the sliced mushrooms and saute for 1 minute. Remove from fire. Keep aside.
5. To prepare the cheese sauce, heat the butter and add the flour. Stir on low heat for 1 minute.
6. Add milk and stir well. Cook till thick.
7. Add the spinach and mushroom mixture and mix well.
8. Add the grated cheese and season with salt and pepper if required.
9. Pour into a greased oven proof dish and bake in a preheated oven at 180°C/350°F/Gas mark 4 for 20-25 minutes till it turns golden.

Garlic Onion Cheese Flan

Serves 6

PASTRY
150 gm (1¼ cups) flour (maida) - sifted
75 gm (1 tbsp more than ¼ cup) butter - cold
2 tbsp water
¼ tsp salt

TOPPING
2 tbsp oil
4 flakes garlic - crushed
3 large onions - sliced finely
1 tbsp flour (maida) mixed in ½ cup water and ½ cup milk
3 eggs - separated
2 tbsp chopped parsley
½ tsp salt
½ tsp freshly ground pepper
½ cup grated cheese, approx.

1. To make the pastry, sift the flour and salt in a bowl.
2. Add cold butter cut into tiny cubes and rub it with finger tips till it resembles fine bread crumbs. Add ice cold water and gather the flour together to make a dough.
3. Chill the dough in the refrigerator for 30 minutes.
4. Roll out the dough and put in a 8" greased pie tin. Bake it in a preheated oven at 180°C/350°F/Gas mark 4 for about 15 minutes or till very light golden. Keep pastry flan aside.
5. For the topping, fry the crushed garlic in the oil. Add sliced onions and fry till transparent. Cool. Keep aside.
6. Mix the flour with milk and water. Add the egg yolks. Add chopped parsley or coriander. Add salt and pepper.
7. Beat egg whites till stiff. Add the whipped egg whites to milk mixture.
8. Cover the baked pastry flan with onions.
9. Top onions with grated cheese nicely.
10. Pour the milk and egg mixture over the cheese.
11. Bake the flan again at 180°C/350°F/Gas mark 4 for ½ hour or till set.

Florets in Broccoli Sauce

Cauliflower and broccoli together in a delightful cheese sauce flavoured and coloured with green broccoli in it.

Picture on page 39   *Serves 5-6*

200 gm (½ of a medium) cauliflower
150 gm (1 small flower) broccoli
1 large carrot - finely chopped
juice of ½ lemon
2 tbsp butter - softened
3-4 flakes garlic - crushed, 1 onion - cut into half and then into rings
¼ tsp salt, ¼ tsp peppercorns (saboot kali mirch) - crushed
2 tbsp grated cheese

BROCCOLI SAUCE
3 tbsp butter - softened
1 tiny flower of broccoli - scraped with a knife from the top to get 1 cup very fine
pieces (like crumbs) of broccoli (do not use the stalk)
3 tbsp plain flour (maida), 3 cups milk
2 tbsp grated cheese
¾ tsp salt and ¼ tsp pepper, or to taste

1. Cut cauliflower and broccoli into medium florets with small stalks.
2. Boil 5-6 cups water with 2 tsp salt, 1 tsp sugar and juice of ½ lemon. Add florets and carrots to boiling water. When a proper boils comes, remove from fire. Leave vegetables in hot water for 2 minutes. Drain. Do not over cook. Refresh in cold water. Strain. Pat dry on a clean kitchen towel or a paper napkin.
3. Pick up the cauliflower and broccoli florets and keep on a plate.
4. Heat butter. Add garlic and onions. Cook till onions turn golden. Add both the florets. Add salt and pepper. Saute, stirring very little, till brown specs appear on the cauliflower. Transfer to an oven proof serving dish.
5. Sprinkle carrots over the florets in the dish. Sprinkle 2 tbsp cheese and some crushed peppercorns on the vegetables.
6. To prepare the sauce, melt butter in a heavy bottomed pan. Add broccoli. Stir for 2 minutes. Add flour. Cook on slow fire for 1-2 minutes.
7. Add milk gradually, stirring continuously. Stir till it boils. Cook for 2-3 minutes. Do not make it too thick. Add 2 tbsp cheese. Add salt and pepper to taste. Remove from fire.
8. Spread the broccoli sauce over the vegetables. Bake at 200°C/475°F for 20 minutes till light brown. Serve immediately.

Rice Aubergine Casserole

A complete Continental meal by itself.

Picture on page 59   Serves 4

1 cup rice
2 bay leaves (tej patta), 1 tsp black cumin (shah jeera)
1 large round brinjal or aubergine (bharte waala baingan) - cut into 1" pieces
1 large capsicum - cut into ½" pieces
oil for frying

RED SAUCE
2 tbsp oil
1½ onions - chopped, 4 large (400 gm) tomatoes - pureed
1 tsp oregano, 1¼ tsp salt, ¼ tsp pepper, ¼ tsp red chilli powder, ½ tsp sugar

CHEESE SAUCE
2 tbsp butter - softened, 2 tbsp plain flour (maida)
2 cups milk, 2 cubes (50 gm) cheese - grated
¾ tsp salt, ¼ tsp pepper

1. Sprinkle 3/4 tsp salt on the brinjal pieces. Mix and keep aside for ½ hour to sweat. Pat dry the aubergine pieces on a paper napkin or kitchen towel. Heat oil and deep fry till golden brown. Keep aside.
2. To boil rice, boil 5-6 cups of water with 1 tsp salt, bay leaves and black cumin. Wash and add rice. Cook till tender. Strain excess water. Run a fork through the hot rice to separate the rice grains. Keep aside.
3. To prepare the red sauce, heat oil. Add chopped onion. Cook till it turns light brown. Add the pureed tomatoes. Add sugar, salt, pepper, red chilli powder and oregano. Cook for about 5 minutes till slightly thick. Remove from heat.
4. For the cheese sauce, heat butter in a clean pan. Add flour and stir on low heat for 1 minute. Add milk and stir continuously till it comes to a boil. Cook for about 2 minutes till it coats the spoon well. Remove from heat. Add cheese, salt & pepper. The sauce should be thin.
5. To assemble, spread half the cooked rice in a medium oven-proof dish. Spread half the aubergines and the chopped capsicum on the rice. Top the brinjals with half the red sauce. Sprinkle half of the white sauce.
6. Again spread rice, then brinjals and then red sauce. Top with white sauce and lastly spread capsicums. Cover the dish with an aluminium foil and bake in a preheated oven for 10 minutes at 200°C. Uncover the casserole and bake further for 5 minutes. Serve hot.

Potato Nests

Serves 4

½ cup boneless chicken pieces
½ kg (4 big) potatoes - boiled and grated
½ cup sliced mushrooms
4 tbsp butter - softened, 2 tbsp milk
a few sprigs coriander leaves
salt and pepper - to taste

1. Mash the boiled potatoes until smooth.
2. Beat in 2 tbsp butter and 2 tbsp milk and season with salt and pepper.
3. With the help of a katori or with your hands make small nests.
4. Cover the back of a baking dish with aluminium foil. Grease it with oil. Place the nests on it. Bake in a preheated oven at 200°C/400°F/Gas mark 6 for 15-20 minutes or until golden.
5. Melt 1 tbsp butter and fry the chicken till golden. Add some water and cook covered till done. Add salt and pepper and dry the chicken. Remove from kadhai. Heat 1 more tbsp oil in the kadhai and saute the mushrooms till golden.
6. Cut the chicken into thin strips like straws. Fill in the potato nests with mushroom and chicken mixture. Garnish with coriander leaves.

Crunchy Baked Fish

Ready made packets of soup add great flavour to baked dishes!

Serves 4

250 gm (4) fish fillets
½ packet mushroom soup
½ cup grated cheese
4 tbsp butter - softened
2 flakes garlic - crushed, 1 onion - grated
1 tsp worcestershire sauce
250 gm potato chips (readymade) - crushed

1. Prepare the mushroom soup according to the instructions, but add half the quantity of water. Cook the soup till it becomes thick like a sauce.
2. Grease a glass oven proof dish, put the fillets.
3. Spread the thick soup and sprinkle the cheese.
4. Fry the garlic and grated onion in butter for 2 minutes. Add worcestershire sauce & ½ tsp salt. Mix well. Spread it over the cheese.
5. Spread crushed potato chips over the onion.
6. Bake at 180°C/350°F/Gas mark 4 for 30-35 minutes.

Tomato Fish

Serves 6

½ kg fish fillets or one big piece of fish
6 large tomatoes - put in boiling water for 3 minutes, peeled & pureed
4 tbsp oil
4 flakes garlic - crushed
1 tsp sugar, 1½ tsp salt, ½ tsp pepper
2 tsp lemon juice

1. Blanch the tomatoes by putting them in boiling water for 3 minutes. Remove the skin and puree them in a mixer.
2. Heat 4 tbsp oil, add crushed garlic, sugar, 1 tsp salt, pepper and the lemon juice. Add the fresh tomato puree and cook till the sauce is thick.
3. Pour half the sauce in a greased baking dish and arrange the fillets on top. Sprinkle ½ tsp salt on the fish. Pour the rest of the tomato sauce.
4. Bake at 180°C/350°F/Gas 4 for 30 minutes or till the fish is done.

Crepes Florentine

The word "florentine "suggests the presence of spinach in the dish. We have pancakes filled with spinach and smothered with some sauce.

Serves 8

10-12 PANCAKES
**1 cup flour (maida), 1¾ cups milk, approx.
1 tsp salt, ½ tsp pepper, ¼ tsp soda-bi-carb (mitha soda)**

WHITE SAUCE
**2 tbsp butter - softened, 2 tbsp flour (maida), 1¾ cups milk
¾ tsp salt and ½ tsp pepper, or to taste**

STUFFING
**2 tbsp butter - softened
1½ onions - chopped finely
500 gm (3 cups finely chopped) spinach
200 gm mushrooms
2 tbsp grated cheese or cheese spread
2 tbsp thick cream
salt and red chilli powder to taste**

OTHER INGREDIENTS
**50 gm mozzarella or pizza cheese - grated
1 tomato - cut into slices & parsley or mint sprigs for garnishing**

1. To prepare the pancakes, sift maida, salt, pepper and soda-bi-carb together.
2. Add milk gradually. Mix well with an egg beater. Add enough milk to get a thin pouring consistency.
3. Heat a non stick pan. Smear 1 tsp oil in the centre. Remove pan from fire and pour 1 karchhi of batter.
4. Tilt the pan to spread the batter very thinly. Return to fire and cook till the under side gets done. Remove pancake from pan. (Cook only one side, do not turn the pancake). Make thin, medium size (6" diameter) pancakes. Similarly make all the pancakes and keep aside.
5. To prepare the white sauce, melt butter and add flour. Stir for a minute on low flame. Add milk, stirring continuously. Add salt and pepper to taste. Cook till it starts to coat the spoon. Remove from flame. Do not make it too thick.
6. For the filling, remove the hard stems of the spinach and chop finely. Cut 2-3 mushrooms into neat paper thin slices for garnishing and keep aside. Chop the rest of the mushrooms into small pieces.

7. Heat butter in a large pan or kadhai. Add onion. Saute for 1 minute. Add the chopped mushrooms. Add ½ tsp salt and ¼ tsp pepper and cook for 3-4 minutes till all the juices drawn from mushrooms evaporate.
8. Add the spinach. Cook till dry. Remove from heat.
9. Add the grated cheese or cheese spread and cream. Mix well. Add a little salt and red chilli powder to taste.
10. To assemble, divide the filling into 10-12 heaps, according to the number of pancakes prepared. Take a pancake. Spread one part of the filling on half the pancake and fold over. Fold again into half to get triangles. Repeat this with all pancakes.
11. Take a shallow rectangular oven proof dish. Spread 1/3 of the white sauce. Arrange the pancakes, slightly overlapping each other.
12. Leaving ½" inch from both sides, pour the remaining white sauce on the pancakes on the centre portion.
13. Arrange tomato slices in a row on the pancakes. Arrange a few paper thin slices of mushrooms on the tomatoes. Sprinkle pizza cheese.
14. At serving time, bake in a preheated oven at 180°C/350°F for 15 minutes. Garnish with parleys or mint sprigs and serve hot.

Italian Tomatoes

Whole blanched tomatoes in a delicious sauce make a good accompaniment to the main meal.

Serves 6

6 medium sized tomatoes - blanched
2 tbsp olive oil
1 tsp ginger paste, 1 tsp garlic paste
1 tsp sugar
¾ cup tomato sauce, 2 tbsp chilli sauce
1 tbsp oregano, ½ cup grated cheese
¾ tsp salt, ¼ tsp pepper

1. Blanch tomatoes in hot water and remove the skin. Keep whole tomatoes aside.
2. Heat oil and fry the ginger and garlic paste.
3. Add tomato sauce, chilli sauce, sugar, salt and pepper.
4. Place the whole tomatoes in an oven proof dish and pour over the sauce over them. Sprinkle oregano and grated cheese.
5. Bake in a preheated oven at 180°C/350°F/Gas mark 4 for 25-30 minutes.

Mushroom Wraps

Make the pancakes for the outer covering well in advance. Convert them into wraps and top them with spinach sauce.

Picture on facing page   *Serves 4*

¾ cup plain flour (maida), 1¼ cups milk, approx.
½ tsp salt, ¼ tsp pepper, a pinch of baking powder

FILLING
1½ tbsp oil, ¼ of an onion - chopped (2 tbsp)
1 cup finely chopped mushrooms
2 tbsp finely chopped cabbage
½ tsp ginger-garlic paste, 1 green chilli - chopped
¼ tsp salt, 2 pinches pepper, or to taste
3-4 tbsp grated cheese (1 cube)

SPINACH SAUCE
2 tbsp butter - softened, 2 tbsp maida
1½ cups very finely chopped spinach
2 cups milk
salt, pepper to taste

OTHER INGREDIENTS
1 tbsp tomato sauce mixed with 1 tsp red chilli sauce
2-3 tbsp grated cheese

1. Sift maida, baking powder & salt. Add pepper. Add milk and beat well to get a smooth pouring consistency. Keep aside for 10 minutes.
2. Heat a non-stick frying pan (not too hot). Put 1 tsp oil on it. Sprinkle a pinch of salt on the pan. Spread the oil and salt with a wooden spoon. Remove from fire and pour 1/3 cup (1½ big karchhi) batter.
3. Tilt the pan to spread the batter to get a thin pancake. Return to fire. Turn the pancake when the edges turn brown. Cook the other side for 1 minute, remove from pan. Make 3-4 such pancakes.
4. For the filling, heat 1½ tbsp oil. Add onions and cook till it turns soft. Add mushrooms and cook further for 2-3 minutes. Add green chillies & ginger-garlic paste. Mix well and add the cabbage. Stir fry on medium flame for 2 minutes. Add salt, pepper to taste. Remove from fire. Add cheese and keep filling aside.
5. Spread a pancake on a flat work place with the light coloured side up. Spread 1 tsp of tomato sauce & chilli sauce mix. Put 2 tbsp of filling in a row at the top.

Contd...

Rice Aubergine Casserole : Recipe on page 53, Mushroom Wraps ➤

Then roll the pancake to get a long roll, sealing the end with tomato sauce. Keep it flat with the joint side down. Neaten the edges by cutting them straight. Cut the roll into 3 pieces to get smaller rolls of about 1½-2" length. Keep the rolls aside.

6. For the sauce, heat 2 tbsp butter in a heavy bottomed kadhai. Add 1½ cups finely chopped spinach and stir for about 2-3 minutes till the water dries. Add maida and stir for ½ minute. Add milk and stir continuously till it boils. Add ¾ tsp salt and ¼ tsp pepper. Simmer on low heat for 3-4 minutes to get a thin pouring sauce which coats the spoon. Remove from fire.

7. Spread ¼ of the sauce in a rectangular serving dish. Arrange the rolls on top. Spread the remaining sauce on top to cover the rolls completely.

8. Grate cheese on top. Bake at 200°C for 10-12 minutes. Serve.

Sweet & Sour Cabbage

A Chinese style of baking cabbage.

Serves 8

1 medium cabbage (about ½ kg) - cut into 1" squares
4 tomatoes
½ cup grated carrot (1 big)
3 tbsp oil
2 tbsp cornflour
1 cup water
2 tbsp vinegar
1 tbsp soya sauce
1 tbsp sugar
2 tsp salt, or to taste

1. Put tomatoes in boiling water for 3-4 minutes. Remove from water and remove the skin and chop.

2. Heat oil and fry the grated carrot and chopped tomatoes for about 5 minutes.

3. Blend in a mixer. Remove from mixer to a bowl.

4. To the tomatoes add vinegar, sugar, soya sauce and salt and mix well.

5. Mix cornflour in 1 cup of water and add to the tomato mixture. Keep it on fire and cook till the mixture is thick and translucent.

6. Cut cabbage into 1" squares.

7. In a greased glass baking dish put the cabbage pieces.

8. Pour over the sweet and sour sauce. Mix gently.

9. Bake in a preheated oven for 20-25 minutes or till the cabbage is done.

Home made Crusty Pizza

Makes 3

THIN CRUSTY HOME MADE PIZZA BASE
¼ cup lukewarm water, ½ tsp sugar
2 tsp heaped dried yeast (10 gms)
¾ cup milk, 1½ tbsp refined oil, 1 tsp salt, 1 tsp sugar
300 gms flour (maida)

TOMATO SAUCE
250 gm tomatoes - blanched (put in hot water and peeled) and chopped finely
½ cup ready made tomato puree
4-5 flakes garlic - crushed
1 tsp dried oregano, 1 bay leaf, 1 tsp vinegar
salt and freshly ground pepper to taste, 1 tsp oil

TOPPING
1 cup capsicum - diced, 200 gm mozzarella (pizza) cheese - grated (2 cups)

1. Mix warm water and sugar in a cup. Feel the water with a finger to check if it is lukewarm. Add yeast. Shake the cup gently to mix the yeast. Cover it and leave it in a warm place till the granules of the yeast disappear and it becomes frothy. (10-15 minutes). (If it does not swell, discard it!).

2. Mix milk, oil, salt and sugar in a pan. Keep aside. When the yeast becomes frothy, heat this milk mixture to make it lukewarm. Add the ready yeast mix to the luke warm milk mixture. Add this yeast and milk mixture to the maida and knead well to make a smooth dough. Grease a big polythene, brush the dough with a little oil and put it in the polythene. Keep it covered in a warm place to swell for 1 hour or till it is double in size. Now punch it down to its original size, brush with oil and keep it back in the polythene for another 15 minutes or till it swells again. Make 3 balls. Flatten each on a 10" square greased aluminium foil to a thin round pizza, even thinner than ¼". Prick each base with a fork. Brush pizza base with butter or olive oil. Bake in a preheated oven at 180°C/350°F/ Gas mark 4 for 15 to 20 minutes.

3. For the tomato sauce, heat oil in a pan. Add garlic. Stir and immediately add all other ingredients of the sauce. Bring to a boil. Lower heat and simmer on low heat for 7-8 minutes, stirring occasionally until it is reduced in quantity and thick enough to spread without being runny. Add the chopped capsicums. Remove sauce from fire. Pour the mixture over the baked pizza base. Cover with grated cheese and sprinkle oregano. Bake for 10-15 minutes or till cheese melts.

Calzone

Calzones are a speciality of Italy. It is a small pizza which is folded over to enclose a filling.

Picture on page 99   *Gives 8-10*

DOUGH
2-3 tbsp lukewarm water, ¼ tsp sugar
1 tsp heaped dried yeast (5 gms)
½ teacup milk, 1 tbsp refined oil, ¾ tsp salt, ½ tsp sugar
150 gms (1 cup plus 2 tbsp) maida (plain flour)

FILLING
2 tbsp oil, 1 onion - chopped fine or 2-3 spring onions - chopped
1 capsicum - chopped very finely, 1 cup chopped mushrooms
2 tsp vinegar, 4 tbsp fresh coriander or parsley - chopped
5-6 tbsp grated cheese (50 gm)
½ tsp salt, ¼ tsp pepper, ½ tsp red chilli flakes

1. For the dough, mix warm water and sugar in a cup. Feel the water with a finger to check if it is lukewarm. Add yeast. Shake the cup gently to mix the yeast. Cover it and leave it in a warm place till the granules of the yeast disappear and it becomes frothy. (10-15 minutes). (If it does not swell, discard it).

2. Mix milk, oil, salt and sugar in a pan. Keep aside. When the yeast becomes frothy, heat this milk mixture to make it lukewarm. Add the ready yeast mix to the luke warm milk mixture.

3. Add this yeast and milk mixture to the maida and knead well to make a smooth dough. Grease a big polythene, brush the dough with a little oil and put it in the polythene. Keep it covered in a warm place to swell for 1 hour or till it is double in size. Now punch it down to its original size, brush with oil and keep it back in the polythene for another 15 minutes or till it swells again.

4. For the filling, heat 2 tbsp oil, add onions. Stir fry till transparent.

5. Add chopped mushrooms. Stir fry for 1-2 minutes.

6. Add capsicum. Stir for a few seconds. Add parsley or coriander, salt, pepper, red chilli flakes and vinegar. Mix well and remove from heat. Add cheese. Cool.

7. Divide dough into 16 marble sized balls. Roll out one portion into a thin chappatti of about 4-5" diameter. Put some filling in the center. Brush the edges with water and fold over to enclose the filling. Press the edges well with a fork to seal. Repeat with the remaining dough.

8. Place the calzone on a greased tray and brush with a little oil or melted butter.

9. Bake in a preheated oven at 180°C/350°F for 15-20 minutes or till golden brown and crisp. Serve hot brushed with some melted butter.

Onion & Capsicum Hot Dogs

Simple, yet delicious!

Serves 4

4 hot dog breads (long buns)
1 capsicum - finely chopped
1 onion - finely chopped
100 gm pizza cheese (mozzarella) - grated (1 cup)

SAUCE
4 large tomatoes
5-6 flakes garlic - crushed or 1 tsp garlic paste
1 tsp sugar
½ tsp vinegar
¾ tsp salt, ½ tsp pepper
1 tsp dried oregano
2 tbsp oil

1. To make the sauce, blanch the tomatoes by putting them in hot water for 7-8 minutes. Remove the skin. Puree the tomatoes in a mixer.
2. Heat oil and fry the garlic. Add the fresh tomato puree and add sugar, vinegar, salt, pepper and oregano. Boil. Cook for about 10 minutes on low heat, till the sauce is thick enough to spread without being runny.
3. Mix onion and capsicum together in a bowl. Add a little salt and pepper to it.
4. Cut the hot dog bread from the middle into two and put them on a greased baking tray or wire rack.
5. Spread sauce. On the sauce spread chopped onions and capsicums.
6. Sprinkle cheese uniformly over it.
7. Bake at 200°C/400°F/Gas mark 6 for 10 minutes or till cheese melts and bread turns a little crisp.

Corn & Mushroom Quiche

Individual quiches prepared in small baking moulds also look wonderful! You can substitute corn with finely chopped and boiled french beans or boiled and shredded chicken.

Picture on page 99   *Serves 6*

SHELL
¼ cup melted butter
1¼ cups plain flour (maida), a big pinch of baking powder
¼ cup grated cheese, 3 tbsp water, or as required

VEGETABLES FOR FILLING
½ cup corn kernels - frozen or tinned or beans, 2 cups sliced mushrooms
¼ tsp salt and ¼ tsp pepper, 1 tbsp butter - softened

MIX TOGETHER
4 tbsp cream, 1½ tbsp tomato puree, 1½ tbsp cornflour
½ tsp salt, ¼ tsp freshly ground pepper
2 tbsp chopped fresh parsley or coriander

OTHER INGREDIENTS
1½ cups (150 gm) grated mozzarella or pizza cheese
½ tsp dried oregano, a few tomato slices

1. Sift flour and baking powder. Combine butter with flour, rubbing well until it looks like bread crumbs. Add cheese. Add just enough water to bind and knead lightly to a firm dough. Chill the dough, well covered in a wet muslin cloth, for 15 minutes.

2. Roll out to a thin chappati, slightly bigger than the baking flan tin (a shallow tin with a loose bottom.) Roll out and place it in the baking flan tin. Press the mixture well to cover the base and the sides too. Press carefully to get a well levelled base. Trim the excess by rolling a rolling pin on the edges of the tin.

A 9" flan tin with a loose (removable) bottom.

Press the rolled out dough into the flan tin.

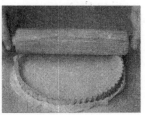

To trim off the excess dough, simply roll a rolling pin over the edges of the flan tin. The rim will act as a cutting edge and the excess will fall away.

3. Prick with a fork all over to avoid the crust from puffing up during baking.
4. Bake the quiche crusts in a hot oven (200°C/390°F), for about 10-15 minutes, until light golden yellow. Allow to cool.
5. To prepare the filling, heat butter. Add mushrooms and cook until water evaporates and they turn dry. Add corn. Add ¼ tsp salt and ¼ tsp pepper. Cook for a few seconds. Remove from fire.
6. In a cup, mix together — cream, tomato puree, cornflour, salt, pepper and parsley.
7. Spoon the mushroom-corn mix into a cooled quiche crust and level it.
8. Sprinkle ¼ cup grated cheese on it, keeping some for the top.
9. Spread the cream-tomato puree mixture on the cheese. Sprinkle with the remaining cheese. Sprinkle some oregano. Arrange a few halved slices of tomato.
10. Bake in a preheated oven set at 190°C/375°F for about 25 minutes or until the filling is set and the top is golden. Allow to cool before serving.

Chicken Parcels

Serves 4

4 chicken breasts - cut into bite sized (1" pieces)
1 onion - sliced
1 cup mushrooms - sliced
2 tsp lemon juice
3-4 tbsp butter - softened
1 tsp salt, ½ tsp pepper

1. Marinate the chicken pieces in 1 tsp salt and ½ tsp pepper for ½ hour.
2. Heat 4 tbsp butter and fry the chicken on a low fire till golden.
3. Take a square aluminium foil and place the chicken in the middle.
4. Mix onions and mushrooms and add salt and pepper to taste. Place some sliced onions and mushrooms with the chicken pieces on the foil.
5. Sprinkle lemon juice and dot with butter and fold the foil to make it as a parcel.
6. Put the parcel on a baking tray and bake it in a preheated oven at 200°C/400°F/ Gas mark 6 for 30-45 minutes.
7. To serve, open the foil slightly to expose the chicken and place on a serving plate.

Chilly Chicken Pizza

Picture on page 69   *Makes 2*

2 ready-made pizza bases or prepare base as given for home made crusty pizza on page 61

150 gm pizza cheese - grated

TOMATO SPREAD
1-2 tbsp oil
4 flakes garlic - crushed and chopped finely
½ tsp red chilli paste or powder
½ cup ready made tomato puree, 2 tbsp tomato sauce
1 tsp oregano (dried), salt and pepper to taste

CHILLI CHICKEN TOPPING
1 boneless chicken breast (100 - 150 gm) - cut into ¼" pieces
1 tsp red chilli paste (or degi mirch), 1 tsp soya sauce, 1 tsp vinegar
a pinch of ajinomoto (optional), ¼ tsp each - salt, pepper
2 tbsp cornflour/maida
½ onion - chopped, 1 small capsicum - chopped, a few olives - sliced, optional

1. To prepare the tomato spread, heat oil on medium heat in a non stick pan. Add garlic. Stir and add tomato puree and sauce, salt & pepper. Add chilli paste or powder. Simmer for 2-3 minutes. Add oregano. Remove from heat.

2. For the chilli chicken topping, cut the chicken breast into ¼" bit pieces. In a bowl marinate with chilli paste or powder, soya sauce, vinegar, salt, pepper and ajinomoto for ½ hour or even more.

3. Heat oil in a kadhai. Drain the extra marinade from chicken pieces. Sprinkle flour and mix well to coat. Fry on medium heat till crisp and light brown in 2 batches. Remove from oil.

4. Add 1 tbsp of the prepared tomato spread to the chicken pieces to keep the chicken succulent and not turn too dry while grilling.

5. To assemble, spread tomato spread on the pizza base, leaving the edges a little. Sprinkle most of the cheese on the tomato spread (reserve a little for the top). Spread chilli chicken, chopped capsicum, onions and olives. Sprinkle the remaining cheese.

6. Place the pizza on the wire rack of a hot oven at 180°C. Grill for about 10 minutes till the base gets crisp (to get a pan (crisp) pizza, oil the base from below, before grilling.) Serve hot with chilli flakes and mustard sauce.

Tea Time
CAKES

Cup used to measure both solids and liquids in the following recipes is the American measuring cup of 8 oz (250 ml). The cup has markings of ¼ cup, ½ cup, ¾ cup and also 1/3 and 2/3 cup, which makes the measuring of ingredients very easy. The measuring cup is easily available in all stores which keep kitchen equipment. In the absence of a measuring cup, a normal big sized coffee mug can be used.

Practical Conversions

AMERICAN CUP (8 OZ, 250 ML)	WEIGHT
1 cup flour	125 gm
1 cup powdered sugar	150 gm
1 cup ordinary sugar	200 gm
1 cup softened butter	250 gm
1 cup grated cheese	100 gm
1 cup oil	250 ml

To measure, place the cup on a flat surface. Fill the ingredient and then level it. For measuring butter, press the softened butter into the cup so that air spaces are forced out.

Coffee Cake

A delicious coffee flavoured cake, topped with chocolate sauce and crunchy almonds.

Makes 10 slices

1½ cups flour (maida)
1½ tsp baking powder
3 eggs - separated
¾ cup butter - softened
¾ cup sugar
2 tbsp instant coffee
1/3 cup water
2 tbsp rum or brandy, optional

TO DECORATE
some ready made chocolate sauce (Hersheys)
12-15 almonds or cashews - crushed coarsely with a rolling pin (belan)

1. Grease and dust a 9" ring pan or a 7" round cake tin.
2. Mix sugar, coffee and water in a big pan. Heat till sugar dissolves. Remove from fire. Keep aside to cool. Add rum or brandy if using.
3. Sieve flour with baking powder.
4. Beat egg whites till stiff and keep aside.
5. Beat butter and egg yolks until creamy.
6. Add the sugar-coffee syrup.
7. Stir in the sifted flour.
8. Fold egg whites into the mixture in two batches. Fold gently till well mixed.
9. Transfer to a greased and dusted tin. Level the top of the mixture first and then make a slight depression in the mixture in the center portion, by shifting some of the mixture in the centre to the sides.
10. Bake in a moderate oven at 180°C/350°F/Gas mark 4, for 40 minutes or till firm. Transfer to a serving platter.
11. Squeeze some chocolate sauce on the sides and swirl all over the top of the cake too.
12. Toast the nuts in a non stick pan or a kadhai till light golden. Sprinkle nuts on the top and serve.

Chilli Chicken Pizza : Recipe on page 66 ➢
Date & Nut Loaf with Toffee Sauce : Recipe on page 87 ➢

Banana Walnut Cake

Makes 8-10 slices

1 cup mashed ripe bananas
½ cup walnuts - crushed coarsely with a rolling pin (belan)
2 cups flour (maida)
1 tsp baking powder
½ tsp soda-bi-carb
½ tsp salt
1 cup powdered sugar
1/3 cup butter (85 gm) - softened
2 eggs
3 tbsp curd

1. Grease a 9" tin. Preheat the oven at 375°F/190°C/Gas mark 4.
2. Sieve flour, baking powder, soda-bi-carb and salt together. Keep aside.
3. Mix walnuts with the flour.
4. Beat sugar and butter very well till creamy.
5. Add eggs to the sugar-butter mixture one at a time.
6. Add mashed bananas and curd. Mix well.
7. Fold in the flour lightly.
8. Pour the mixture in a greased tin and bake for 50-60 minutes, check by inserting a knife or a tooth pick in the middle of the cake, it should come out clean.
9. Cool for 10 minutes and remove from the tin.
10. Sift icing sugar on top through a sieve. (see below)

Use strips of paper to make a striped pattern. Lay the strips on the cake, criss-crossing if you like. Sprinkle icing sugar through a fine sieve, then lift off the paper carefully so as not to disturb the pattern.

Apple & Date Cake

A wonderful combination!

Makes 8-10 slices

Picture on page 1

2 large apples - peeled, cored and chopped
1/3 cup butter - softened (85 gm)
1 cup powdered sugar
2 eggs
2 tsp baking powder
1¾ cups flour (maida)
½ cup walnuts - chopped
1 cup dates - stoned and chopped

1. Blend apples to a puree with 4 tbsp water.
2. Sift flour with baking powder. Keep aside.
3. Beat the butter and sugar in a pan nicely till light and fluffy.
4. Alternately add the eggs and sieved flour to the butter.
5. Add the apple puree. Mix.
6. Keeping aside 1 tbsp each of dates and walnuts for the top, add the rest of the walnuts and dates to the cake mixture. Mix well.
7. Grease and dust a big rectangular loaf tin of 11"x4" or a round 9" diametre cake tin. Spoon the mixture in the tin and bake in a preheated oven at 180°C/350°F/ Gas mark 4, for about 1 hour or till done.
8. Cool for 5 minutes before removing the cake from the tin.

Cardamom Cake

A crunchy sugary topping with a lovely flavour of cardamoms.

Makes 10-12 slices

1½ cups plus 1 tbsp (200 gm) flour
¾ cups (140 gm) oil
¾ cup (160 gm) ordinary sugar
4 eggs - yolks & whites separated
2 tsp level baking powder
½ tsp ground (seeds of 3 pieces) cardamom seeds (moti illaichi)
½ cup curd

TOPPING
2 tbsp sugar, preferably brown
10-12 almonds or cashewnuts - crushed roughly
½ tsp ground (seeds of 3 pieces) cardamom seeds (moti illaichi)

1. Separate whites of eggs in a small pan and the yolks in a small bowl.
2. Beat egg whites till stiff.
3. Sift flour, baking powder and ground cardamom seeds together and keep aside.
4. Beat sugar and oil together in a pan for a few minutes.
5. Add the egg yolks. Mix well.
6. Add half of the flour (maida) and half of the curd in the mixture. Beat well.
7. Add the left over maida & the curd. Beat well.
8. Fold the egg whites with a wooden spoon, with an upward and downward motion till the egg whites get mixed with the cake batter.
9. Grease an 8" x 8" square cake tin or a 9" round tin and pour the cake batter 1" high into it.
10. Mix together - 2 tbsp of sugar, almonds or kaju and cardamom powder. Sprinkle on the top.
11. Bake in a preheated oven at 180°C/350°F for 40 minutes.

Cherry Almond Cake

The cake is festive enough for a formal tea.

Makes 8 slices

3/4 cup plus 1 tbsp (100 gm) flour (maida)
1/3 cup (65 gm) oil
2/3 cups (100 gm) powdered sugar
2 eggs
1 tsp baking powder
¼ cup glace cherries - cut into round slices
½ cup almonds - chopped roughly
2-3 drops almond essence

1. Grease and dust with flour, an 8" x 4" loaf tin.
2. Preheat oven to 150°C/300°F.
3. Sieve flour and baking powder and keep aside in a shallow bowl.
4. Keeping aside a few cherries and almonds for the top, lightly mix the rest of chopped fruit (cherries and almonds) with the sieved flour.
5. Beat sugar and eggs in a pan till frothy.
6. Add oil gradually and keep beating all the time.
7. Add the flour to the egg batter. Mix well.
8. Add essence and mix well. The batter is quite thick but it should be such that you can spoon it out.
9. Put into the prepared tin. Sprinkle the chopped fruit on top.
10. Bake in the preheated oven at 150°C/300°F for 1 hour.
11. When the cake is done, remove from oven. Let it cool for 10 minutes and then remove from the tin. Cut into slices to serve.

Carrot & Date Cake

A soft and moist cake, easy to make in a liquidizer.

Picture on back cover   *Make 10-12 slices*

2 carrots - grated (1½ cups)
1 cup dates - shredded
4 eggs
2½ cups flour (maida)
2 tsp baking powder
1 tsp spices - nutmeg, cinnamon and cloves powder
½ tsp vanilla essence
2 cups powdered sugar
1 cup refined oil
½ cup sugar - to caramelize

1. Grease a 9" round tin or 2 loaf tin. Preheat the oven at 375°F/190°C/Gas mark 4.
2. Whisk egg whites in a dry liquidizer and then add the yellow.
3. Add oil and mix.
4. Add powdered sugar and mix.
5. Sift flour with baking powder. Add flour, spices and essence to the liquidizer.
6. To caramelize, heat a heavy bottomed pan. Add sugar and stir till golden. Remove from fire. Add ¼ cup hot water and mix well. Cook till sugar dissolves. Remove from fire and measure ¼ cup.
7. Add ¼ cup caramelized sugar to the cake batter in the mixer.
8. Add dates and carrots. Mix well.
9. Pour into the greased tin and bake for 50-60 minutes. Check by inserting a skewer in the middle of the cake, it should come out clean.
10. Stand for 10 minutes before turning out the cake.

Orange Marmalade Cake

A very soft, peach coloured cake. Make it in ring cake tin if you like to get a ring cake.

Makes 12-15 slices

2 cups flour (maida)
½ tsp baking powder
½ tsp soda-bi-carb
¼ tsp salt
1½ cups powdered sugar
½ cup butter (125 gm) - softened
3 eggs
1 cup orange marmalade
¼ cup curd mixed with ¼ cup water to get ½ cup butter milk (lassi)

1. Sieve the flour, baking powder, soda-bi-carb and salt.
2. Cream butter and sugar till light and fluffy.
3. Add eggs, one at a time, beating well after each addition.
4. Beat in the marmalade.
5. Add flour alternately with butter milk and beat until mixed well.
6. Pour the mixture in a 9-10" greased cake tin and bake at 180°C/350°F/Gas mark 4 for 25-30 minutes or till done. If you wish to make a ring cake, bake some cake mixture in the ring mould, filling it half and the rest of the mixture can be baked in individual small bowls or even steel katoris will do well.
7. Cool for 5 minutes before removing the cake from the tin.

A ring cake baked in a ring mould.

Low Fat - Yogurt Cake

I was very hesitant to try out this recipe, but the "low fat" words pushed me into it. I am happy I did! Enjoy the cake without guilt!

Makes 8 slices

¾ cup yogurt (dahi)
1 cup powdered sugar
1¼ cups flour (maida)
1 tsp baking powder
2 eggs
5 tbsp oil
1 tbsp vanilla essence
2 tbsp icing sugar - for topping

1. Sift the flour and baking powder.
2. Beat the eggs and oil. Add essence.
3. Beat the sugar with yogurt in a big pan. Keep aside.
4. Add half the egg mixture to the yogurt mixture. Add half the flour and beat well. Add the remaining egg and the flour, beating well till smooth and well mixed.
5. Pour the mixture into a greased 8" cake tin.
6. Bake for 35 - 45 minutes till done in a preheated oven at 180°C/350°F/ Gas mark 4. Cool for 5 minutes and remove the cake from the tin.
7. Sift the icing sugar over the cake. You may make stars or any other pattern by making stencils as shown below.

Simple Cake Stensils

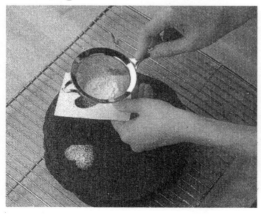

To decorate a cake with stars or other simple shapes, make a stencil by cutting the shape from a square of cardboard (a file folder works well). Hold the stencil over the top of the cake and sift cocoa or icing sugar over it. Repeat for desired pattern.

Dark Chocolate Cake

Extremely simple to prepare. Tastes good plain or with icing and even makes a perfect base for any dessert.

Makes 8-10 slices

4 eggs
1/3 cup cocoa powder
¾ cup powdered sugar
½ cup oil
2/3 cup maida (flour)
1¾ tsp baking powder
¼ tsp soda-bicarb
1 tsp vanilla essence

1. Beat eggs and powdered sugar with an electric egg beater till 4 times in volume and very frothy. If you do not possess an electric beater, beat the eggs and sugar in a pan kept on a smaller pan filled with boiling hot water (double boiler). The eggs are beaten over steam, taking care that the hot water does not touch the pan of eggs.
2. Sift maida, baking powder, cocoa and soda-bicarb. Keep aside.
3. Add the oil gradually to the frothy egg mixture and keep beating slowly. Add essence. Mix.
4. Using a wooden spoon, with an upward and downward motion, fold in maida gradually, a little at a time. Do not over mix. Fold gently.
5. Transfer to a greased round tin of 9" diameter and bake at 180°C/350°F for 30-35 minutes.
6. Test the cake by inserting a clean knife in the centre of the cake.
   If the knife comes out clean, the cake is ready. Remove from the oven.
7. Remove cake from the tin after 5 minutes.

Raisin Cake

Too good to be true! The jaggery topping does a lot to the cinnamon flavoured eggless cake.

Picture on facing page   Makes 8 slices

2 cups flour (maida)
½ tsp cinnamon (dalchini) powder
¼ tsp salt
½ cup butter - melted
½ cup raisins (kishmish)
¾ cup powdered sugar
½ cup milk
½ cup water
1½ tsp white vinegar
1½ tsp soda-bi-carb

TOPPING
2 tbsp jaggery (gur) powder
2 tbsp roughly crushed almonds or oats

1. Sieve flour, cinnamon powder and salt.
2. Add melted butter and mix with the finger tips.
3. Stir in the raisins. Keep aside.
4. Mix together - milk, water, sugar, vinegar and the soda-bi-carb.
5. Add the milk mixture to the flour and beat till well mixed and smooth.
6. Grease an 8" cake tin and dust with flour.
7. Pour the mixture in the tin.
8. Crush the almonds coarsely with the rolling pin (belan). Mix jaggery with the crushed almonds or oats. Sprinkle this mixture on top of the cake.
9. Bake at 180°C/350°F/Gas mark 4 for 35-40 minutes or till done.
10. Cool for 5 minutes before removing the cake.

Walnut Brownies : Recipe on Page 101 ➢
Apple Roll : Recipe on page 106 ➢
Black Forest Cake : Recipe on page 98 ➢
Raisin Cake ➢

Quick Iced Chocolate Cake

Easy to make, this eggless cake made with vinegar is iced with a quick chocolate icing.

Makes 12 slices

1½ cups flour (maida)
4 tbsp cocoa powder
1 tsp soda-bi-carb
1 cup plus 2 tbsp powdered sugar
6 tbsp oil
1 cup milk
1 tsp white vinegar
1 tsp vanilla essence

ICING
2 tbsp butter - melted
6 tbsp cocoa
1 cup icing sugar - sifted
½ tsp vanilla essence
2-3 tbsp hot water

1. Sieve flour, cocoa and soda-bi-carb.
2. Put the flour in a bowl. Add sugar, oil, milk, vinegar and the essence. Mix well.
3. Grease an 8" cake tin and dust it with maida.
4. Pour the mixture and bake at 180°C/350°F/Gas mark 4 for 35-40 minutes or till done.
5. For the icing, melt butter and pour in a mixing bowl. Add cocoa to the melted butter.
6. Sift icing sugar. Add it to the cocoa mixture. Add essence. Mix.
7. Add hot water little by little till the icing has a soft spreading consistency.
8. Spread the icing on a cool cake. Allow to set.

Marble Cake

A two coloured cake. Very simple to prepare, yet good to look at!

Makes 10-12 slices

1 tin condensed milk (400 gm milk maid)
2 cups (250 gm) flour (maida)
2 tbsp sugar
½ cup (125 gm) butter - softened
1½ tsp baking powder
1½ tsp soda-bi-carb
2 tsp vanilla essence
1 cup (250 ml) milk
1 tbsp cocoa powder

1. Grease a 9" round cake tin.
2. Preheat oven to 150°C/300°F.
3. Sieve flour, baking powder & soda-bi-carb together. Keep aside.
4. Mix condensed milk, butter, sugar & essence.
5. Add milk. Mix.
6. Add flour gradually, mixing well after each addition. Beat well for 3-4 minutes till the mixture is light & fluffy.
7. Divide into 2 parts. To one part add cocoa powder and mix well.
8. Put half of the plain mixture in half side of the cake tin. In the other empty half, put half the chocolate mixture. Swirl a spoon lightly in the mixture to get the marble effect.
9. Now, put the left over plain mixture on the chocolate mix and the chocolate one on the plain mixture. Swirl a spoon again.
10. Smoothen the top & bake at 150°C/300°F for 1 hour.
11. Insert a clean knife in the centre of the cake. If it comes out clean, switch off the oven. Remove from oven after 5 minutes.

Orange Cup Cake

Makes 8 cups cakes

1¼ cups flour (maida)
1½ tsp baking powder, ¾ tsp soda-bi-carb
100 gm butter (about ½ cup, less 1 tbsp)
½ cup powdered sugar
½ cup milk
6 tbsp orange squash
2 tbsp cashewnuts (kaju)
2 tbsp raisins (kishmish)

1. Sieve the flour, baking powder and the soda-bi-carb.
2. Beat butter and sugar till light and fluffy.
3. Add the flour, milk and orange squash. Mix well. Add ½ of the nuts and raisins.
4. Pour into the small cake moulds or small steel katoris.
5. Sprinkle the remaining cashewnuts and raisins on top.
6. Bake at 180°C/350°F/Gas mark 4 for 20-25 minutes.

Yogurt Chocolate Cake

An economical and a quick eggless chocolate cake. See that the curd is not sour.

Makes 10 slices

2 cups flour (maida), 1½ tsp baking powder
1 cup sugar, ½ cup butter - softened
1 cup curd
3 tbsp cocoa
1 tsp vanilla essence

1. Sieve the flour and the baking powder.
2. Beat sugar and butter till fluffy.
3. Add the curd, vanilla essence and cocoa and mix well.
4. Lastly add the flour.
5. Pour the mixture into a greased 9" baking tin.
6. Bake in a preheated oven at 180°C/350°F/Gas mark 4 for 35-40 minutes or until done. Remove after 2 minutes.

Fruit Bar

If you do not have mixed spice, just crush 2 cloves and a small piece of cinnamon instead. Bake this cake in a rectangular loaf tin.

Makes 8-10 slices

½ tin milk-maid
1 tbsp sugar
¼ cup (60 gm) unsalted butter - softened
½ cup (125 ml) milk
1 cup (125 gms) maida (plain flour)
½ level tsp soda-bi-carb, 1 tsp baking powder
1 tsp vanilla essence
1/3 cup mixed glace fruit (coloured petha)
2 tbsp chopped cashewnuts
½ tsp mixed spice, (nutmeg, cinnamon and clove powder), optional
few drops of yellow colour

1. Beat milk-maid, sugar and butter together. Add milk, mix well.
2. Sift maida with baking powder and soda-bi-carb.
3. Add the sifted maida gradually to the milk-maid mixture, beating after each addition. Beat well.
4. Add yellow colour and essence. Mix.
5. Keeping aside 1 tbsp of fruits, mix the rest of fruit and cashews with 1 tbsp of maida and add to the cake batter. Beat well till light and fluffy.
6. Transfer to a greased 8" x 4" rectangular loaf tin.
7. Sprinkle some fruits and cashews on top. Bake at 150°C/300°F for 45 minutes.

FANCY PARTY CAKES

Tips on Icing

The cake can also be eggless. Prepare the eggless cake as explained earlier and ice it as given in the following section.

1. Always chill the cream for 15-20 minutes in the freezer before beating it but do not keep it for too long in the freezer, otherwise it will get frozen.
2. The cream should be chilled in the same utensil (pan) in which it is going to be beaten, so that the pan is also cold.
3. Never beat cream in a mixer. Always use either an electric hand mixer or a mechanical hand egg beater.
4. Beat the cream in a cool place or over ice during summers. To do this, place lots of ice cubes in a big pan and place the smaller pan containing the cream over the ice cubes.
5. Beat the cream very carefully otherwise it will turn into butter. The cream first starts getting thick, then comes to the dropping consistency stage and then it forms soft peaks. The peak stage is where one stops beating. The cream is now ready for icing.
6. Never over beat the cream. Once it reaches the peak stage, stop beating immediately. Over beating the cream might make it loose and it may no longer remain stiff.
7. Sometimes, the cream refuses to turn thick on beating. In such cases, add a few drops of lemon juice and chill cream for 10 minutes and then proceed.
8. Chill the ready icing in the refrigerator for 10-15 minutes before use.

For stars, hold the icing bag or gun at 90° angle with the tip slightly above the surface of the cake. Squeeze bag to form a star, then stop squeezing and pull bag away. The size of the star depends on the amount of pressure applied as well as the size of the opening of the bag. For a border, hold the bag at 45° angle and apply equal pressure as you move forward.

Pink Silver Cup Cakes

A sure hit for a children's party! Little girls will love to help their mother decorate the cake with silver balls.

Makes 20-24 cup cakes

1 cup flour (maida)
1½ tsp baking powder
½ cup powdered sugar
½ cup butter - softened
2 eggs
1 tsp vanilla essence
24 small paper cups

FOR THE ROYAL ICING
1 cup icing sugar (approx.) - sifted
1 egg white
a pinch of strawberry or pink colour
½ tsp strawberry essence
2 tbsp silver balls

1. Sieve the flour with baking powder.
2. Beat sugar with butter till light and fluffy.
3. Add egg and flour alternately to the sugar and butter mixture.
4. Add the essence.
5. Place paper cups in deep muffin tins as shown in the picture. Pour a spoonful of mixture in each paper cup, filling it ¾ full. Bake in a preheated oven for 15-20 minutes at 180°C/350°F/Gas mark 4 or till done.
6. To make the icing, beat the egg white till stiff.
7. Add the essence & colour and icing sugar and beat well till mixed.
8. Pour the icing on the cup cakes.
9. Decorate them with silver balls.

Glazed Mocha Fudge Cake

It's just yum!

Picture on page 2

Makes 12 slices

1 cup butter - softened
1½ cups powdered sugar
2 tsp vanilla essence
4 eggs - separated
¾ cup flour (maida)
2 tsp baking powder
1/3 cup cocoa
¾ cup plain yogurt
3 tbsp dry instant coffee mixed with 1 tbsp boiling water

MOCHA GLAZE
4 tbsp cocoa powder
2 tbsp butter - softened
1 tbsp dry instant coffee mixed in 2 tbsp hot water
¾ cup icing sugar - sifted
½ cup chopped walnuts

1. Grease 10" square cake tin.
2. Sift flour, baking powder and cocoa powder together.
3. Separate eggs. Beat egg whites in a clean dry pan until fluffy. Keep aside.
4. Cream butter, sugar and essence with an electric beater until fluffy.
5. Beat in one egg yolk at a time.
6. Add sifted flour, yogurt and coffee mixed with hot water. Mix well.
7. Fold egg whites into the mixture.
8. Bake in a preheated oven at 190°/375°F/Gas mark 5 for 45 minutes. Check by inserting a skewer, it should come out clean.
9. Turn out the cake to cool.

For the mocha glaze : Prepare it after the cake is no longer hot.
1. Boil 2 tbsp water in a pan. Remove from fire. Add cocoa and butter to it.
2. Return to fire and cook stirring over low heat without boiling, until smooth.
3. Add Coffee.
4. Remove from heat and stir in the sifted icing sugar. Mix well.
5. Glaze the cake with the icing, making peaks with the spoon. Decorate it with walnuts
6. Refrigerate until glaze is set.

Date & Nut Loaf
with Toffee Sauce

The toffee sauce made from jaggery gives the final touch to this rich cake.

Makes 8-10 slices   *Picture on page 69*

½ tin milk maid (condensed milk) - 200 gm
1/3 cup oil
250 gm dates
2/3 cup (85 gm) flour (maida)
½ cup walnuts - chopped finely
½ tsp vanilla essence
1 tsp baking powder, ½ tsp soda-bi-carb

TOFFEE SAUCE
½ tbsp butter
4 tbsp jaggery (powdered gur)
5-6 tbsp fresh cream, ½ cup roughly chopped walnuts

1. Remove seeds from dates and chop them finely.
2. Add 6 tbsp of water to the dates and keep on low flame for 2 minutes. Remove from fire. Add ½ tsp soda-bi-carb. Keep aside for 15-20 minutes.
3. Sift maida with baking powder.
4. Mix dates and walnuts with flour.
5. Beat butter and condensed milk very well. Add essence. Mix.
6. Add maida. Beat well. Transfer to a greased loaf tin of size 11"x4".
7. Bake in a preheated oven at 150°C/300°F for 45 minutes.
8. Insert a clean knife in the centre of the cake. If it comes out clean, switch off the oven. Remove from oven after 5 minutes.
9. Unmould on a wire rack. Prick the cake slightly for the sauce to seep in. Place it in the serving plate.

Toffee Sauce:
10. For the sauce, heat butter in a small thick bottomed sauce pan on medium heat.
11. Add the jaggery. Cook for ½ minute till the mixture is frothy. Remove from heat.
12. Add the cream. Return to low heat.
13. Stir for a few seconds till well blended. Do not bring to a boil.
14. Add the walnuts. Remove from fire and pour over the cake kept in the serving platter. Spread to get an even coating of the sauce.

Fresh Fruit Gateau

Picture on facing page   *Makes 8 slices*

CAKE
4 eggs
1 cup maida (flour), 2 tsp baking powder
¾ cup powdered sugar
½ cup oil (refined)
1 tsp vanilla essence

OTHER INGREDIENTS
½ cup orange juice
300 gm fresh cream - chilled, 5 tbsp powdered sugar, 1 tsp vanilla essence
2 tbsp strawberry jam or crush, fresh fruits - strawberries, grapes, chikoos, kiwi etc

1. Sieve flour and baking powder and keep aside.
2. Beat sugar and eggs with a hand or electric beater very well or till the volume is nearly four times. Add essence. Mix.
3. Add oil gradually, beating the mixture all the time.
4. Now add the flour little by little, while you go on beating the mixture on the lowest speed of the electric beater or fold maida very slowly with a spoon, moving the spoon in an upward and downward motion (fold).
5. When all the maida has been added and mixed well, pour into a greased tin 10" diametre and bake in a preheated oven at 300°F/150°C for 30 min. Test the cake by inserting a knife or a skewer. When it comes out clean, switch off the oven.
6. Let the cake cool for 5-10 minutes in the tin before removing from the tin.
7. Cut some fruit into very small pieces to get 1 cup mixed, chopped fruit. Leave most of the fruit for decorating the cake.
8. Cut cake into 2 halves. Soak each piece slightly with orange juice.
9. Beat cream with sugar and essence till thick and soft peaks are formed. Chill. Fill some cream in the icing gun and keep away in the refrigerator.
10. Place a cake piece in a serving plate.
11. Spread 4-5 tbsp of whipped cream over it. Spread some fruit over the cream.
12. Spread some crush or jam on the second piece of cake and invert it on the fruits on the first piece of cake, very carefully. Press well.
13. Cover with cream. Pipe a border at the bottom and top edges with the icing in the gun. Cut some black grapes into halves and press on the sides. Cut strawberries into halves and arrange at the outer border of the cake. Peel and cut chikoo into slices. Cut slices into halves. Fix 2 rows of slices, slightly overlapping the ends of strawberries, keeping them a little upright. Arrange grapes in the center. Chill.

Chocolate Truffle

Rich Chocolate cake iced with a dark chocolate icing.

Makes 10-12 slices

CAKE
4 eggs
1/3 cup cocoa powder
2/3 cup maida (flour)
¾ cup powdered sugar
½ cup oil (refined)
1¾ tsp baking powder
¼ tsp soda-bicarb
1 tsp vanilla essence

CHOCOLATE ICING
150 gm (¾ cup) white butter (cooking butter) - softened
1 cup icing sugar - sifted
½ cup cocoa approx.
½ tsp brandy essence or 1 tsp vanilla essence

ICING FOR THE TOP
½ cup icing sugar - sieved
¼ cup butter or margarine - softened
80 gms bitter chocolate (2 slabs of 40 gms each) - Nestle, Amul, Bournville
¼ cup water
1 egg

1. To prepare the cake, sieve flour, cocoa, soda-bicarb & baking powder together.
2. Beat sugar and eggs with a hand or an electric beater till very frothy.
3. Add oil gradually beating the mixture lightly all the time.
4. Gradually add flour while you go on beating the mixture on the lowest speed of the electric beater or very slowly by hand. Do not over beat.
5. Pour into a greased 8" round tin and bake in a preheated oven at 300°F/150°C for 30-40 minutes. Test the cake by inserting a knife or skewer. When it comes out clean remove immediately from the oven. Let the cake cool for 5-10 minutes in the tin before removing from the tin. Remove from the tin & keep aside.
6. Prepare the chocolate icing by beating the butter till smooth & creamy.
7. Sieve the icing sugar & add to the butter. Beat till fluffy.
8. Add sifted cocoa powder gradually, beating after each addition, till you get the desired colour. Add enough cocoa to get a dark, rich chocolate colour.

9. Fill some icing in an icing gun and keep in the lower shelf of the fridge. Chill the left over icing in the freezer for 5-7 minutes.
10. Cut the cake into 3 parts. Spread ½ of the icing on the first piece of cake.
11. Keep the second piece of cake on top. Spread all the icing. Cover with the last piece of cake. Keep in the fridge.
12. To prepare the icing for the top, heat ¼ cup water in a small heavy bottomed pan, with bitter chocolate (broken into small pieces) on low heat, stirring all the time till chocolate dissolves.
13. Add butter and stir.
14. When butter dissolves remove for heat and add sieved icing sugar. Mix till sugar dissolves.
15. Add egg and immediately stir vigorously, otherwise strands will be made. Heat on low fire, stirring continuously till the icing gets a thick smooth pouring consistency. Do not let boil.
16. Immediately pour over the sandwiched cake. Cover sides with a spatula or knife and leave for 2-3 hours for setting. Pipe a border or any design with the gun.
17. Decorate with chocolate flakes or curls if you like.

Grating Chocolate: Gently rub a lightly chilled bar of chocolate along the coarse edge of a vegetable grater.

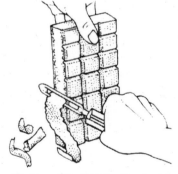

Making Chocolate Curls: Use a vegetable peeler to shave off curls from the side of a block of well chilled chocolate.

Foot Ball Cake

This is an unusual shaped cake which will be a great favourite with little boys. It is baked in a `kadhai` which every Indian household has.

Makes 8 pieces

¾ cup flour (maida)
½ cup butter - softened
½ cup powdered sugar
½ cup cocoa
2 eggs
1½ tsp baking powder
2 tbsp milk

FOR THE ICING
2 cups icing sugar
½ tsp vanilla essence
3 tbsp hot water
½ cup cocoa powder
1 tsp butter - melted

1. Grease a 9" white metal kadhai and sprinkle some flour on it.
2. Beat the sugar and butter till light and fluffy.
3. Sieve the flour and baking powder.
4. Add egg and flour alternately to the mixture.
5. Add the milk.
6. Divide the mixture into two portions.
7. Add sieved cocoa to one portion and beat well.
8. Add spoonfuls of both the mixture alternately into the greased 'kadhai'.
9. Bake in a preheated oven for 35-45 minutes at 180°C/350°F/Gas mark 4 or till done.
10. Cool for the 5 minutes and gently remove the cake on a plate.
11. For the icing, sift the icing sugar. Add essence. Add hot water gradually and beat with a wooden spoon until smooth and glossy. Adjust to just pouring consistency adding more water if required.
12. Divide the icing into two portions.
13. To one portion add cocoa powder and a little butter. Mix well.
14. Make a square pattern on the inverted cake with white and chocolate icing squares alternately.

Orange Chiffon Cake

Makes 10-12 slices   *Picture on cover*

¼ **cup flour (maida), ¼ cup cornflour**
1 tsp baking powder, a pinch of salt
4 eggs
½ cup powdered sugar, 1 tsp vanilla essence

ORANGE ICING
1/3 cup butter - softened, 1 cup icing sugar - sifted
1 tbsp orange rind (explained later)
2 tbsp orange juice (ready made)

OTHER INGREDIENTS
¼ cup orange juice - to soak cake
2 oranges - for decoration
¼ cup sugar - to glaze oranges
50 gm cream - whipped till thick, optional

1. Sieve flour, cornflour, baking powder and salt.
2. Separate the eggs. Beat the egg whites till stiff. Add essence.
3. Add sugar to the egg whites and whisk till thick and smooth. Add the egg yolks.
4. Gently fold in the flour mixture into the eggs. Pour in a 8" greased and dusted cake tin. Bake in a preheated oven at 200°C/400°F/Gas mark 6 for 15 minutes or till done. Cool, remove the cake and cut it horizontally into two parts.
5. For the orange icing, take out orange rind. Scrape the white pith beneath a piece of orange peel by keeping it on a flat surface. Cut it very finely into thin strips.
6. Cream together sugar and butter till light and fluffy.
7. Beat in the orange juice and the rind.
8. Place one piece of cake in a serving platter. Soak it with 4-5 tbsp of orange juice. Spread half the icing on it. Soak the second piece of cake and invert it over the icing. Spread the remaining icing on the top.
9. To garnish with oranges, cut a segment into half widthwise. Slit the segment into two pieces to expose the filling and to get small butterflies. Arrange these in the centre on the iced cake. Pipe a star of whipped cream on it. Cut the orange segments into half lengthwise to separate them into 2 long pieces with the flesh showing and arrange these overlapping, around the edges to form a border.
10. To glaze the oranges, boil ¼ cup sugar with ¼ cup water. Remove from fire after a few seconds. Add a few strips of orange rind for garnishing. After the syrup cools, arrange the orange strips on the whipped cream and brush the oranges with sugar syrup. Serve cold.

Chocolate Temptation

Just can't resist it!

Picture on page 109   *Makes 10-12 slices*

MOIST CAKE
2 large eggs, ¾ cup powdered sugar
2/3 cup ordinary sugar, 2/3 cup curd
1/3 cup cocoa powder, 1 tsp vanilla essence
1½ cups (200 gm) plain flour (maida), 1 tsp soda-bi-carb
½ cup (90 gm) oil

TO SOAK
½ cup cold milk, 1 tbsp sugar, 1 tsp rum or brandy (optional)

CHOCOLATE CREAM FILLING
150 gm cream (¾ cup)
3 tbsp powdered sugar, 3-4 tbsp cocoa
½ tsp vanilla essence

TOPPING
50 gm fresh cream, 1 tsp butter - softened
2 slabs (40 gm each) of - dark Amul, Nestle or Cadburys Bournville chocolate
a packet of nutties

1. Grease an 8-9" round tin. Preheat oven to 180°C/350°F.
2. To prepare the cake, mix ordinary sugar, curd, vanilla essence and cocoa in a large pan. Beat well till sugar dissolves. Keep aside.
3. Beat powdered sugar and eggs till frothy and double in volume.
4. Add oil to the eggs gradually, beating all the time. (see picture)
5. Sift flour and soda-bi-carb together.
6. Add ½ the flour and ½ the beaten eggs to the cocoa mixture in the pan. Mix well. Add the left over flour and eggs and beat well till the mixture is smooth. Bake in the prepared tin at 180°C for 1 hour. Remove from oven. Cool.

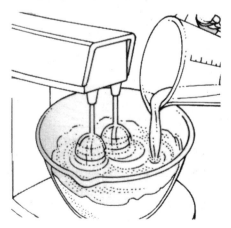

Contd...

7. Remove from tin. Cut through the cake, horizontally into 3 round pieces, with a sawing motion, using a long serrated knife. (See picture)

8. Mix ½ cup of cold milk with 1 tbsp sugar and 1 tsp rum or brandy. Soak each piece of cake with 3 tbsp of this milk. Keep aside to cool.

9. To prepare the filling beat chilled cream with sugar, cocoa and essence till soft peaks form. Beat further very carefully with a spoon till stiff peaks are ready.

10. Place a piece of cake on a serving plate. Spread half of the chocolate cream on it. Invert the second piece of cake on it.

11. Spread the left over cream. Finally place the last piece of cake on it.

12. Press very lightly. Dust the top to get rid of any crumbs. Keep aside.

13. To prepare the topping, break softened chocolates into small pieces. Heat the cream in a small heavy bottomed pan, on low heat (do not boil). Add chocolate pieces and butter and heat stirring continuously, till chocolate melts and you get a smooth paste.

14. Immediately pour over the cake, leaving just a tsp of it. Spread with a long knife dipped in cold water. Keep in the fridge for 30 minutes for the top icing to set.

15. Make crisscross with a fork. Arrange nutties dipped in left over icing.

Hawaiian Cake

Pineapples all the way! Cherries are added to give colour to the cake.

Makes 10-12 slices

1 recipe basic sponge cake - using pineapple essence - page 97
1 small tin of pineapple slices, 1 cup tinned cherries
15 cashews - broken into bits and roasted in a dry pan till golden

ICING
250 gm fresh cream - chilled
6 tbsp powdered sugar
1 tsp pineapple essence

1. Prepare a pineapple sponge cake as given on pages 97, but remember to use 1 tsp of pineapple essence and 1 tsp of vanilla essence, instead of 1½ tsp vanilla essence.

2. Put cream, sugar and essence in a pan. Chill in the freezer for 15-20 minutes. Beat chilled cream till it becomes thick and soft peaks are formed. Put ¼ of the cream in an icing gun and keep in the fridge. Keep the left over cream in the freezer for 15 minutes.

3. Chop 3-4 pineapple slices very finely. Drain and keep aside. Remove seeds from ½ cup cherries.

4. Cool the cake. Cut the cake horizontally into 2 parts.

5. Soak both pieces of cake with pineapple syrup of the tin. Spoon 4-5 tbsp syrup on each piece. Do not make the cake too moist.

6. Spread 2-3 tbsp chilled pineapple icing on the base of the cake.

7. Sprinkle some pineapple bits and stoned cherries all over the cake.

8. Spread very little icing on the second piece of cake, keeping most of the icing for the top. Place the second piece on the first piece of cake with the cream side down. Spread cream icing on the top. Chill.

9. Spread 2 tbsp of icing on the sides. Press finely chopped pineapple on the sides.

10. Pipe a border all round. Pipe stars or swirls on the edges leaving a gap of 1" between the two stars. Put a cherry on each star. Sprinkle the roasted cashews all over in the centre. Cut a pineapple slice into 5-6 pieces and arrange on the cake inbetween the stars, pointing towards the centre.

Note: You may store the left over cherries and pineapple in separate clean plastic boxes in the freezer compartment of your refrigerator for a month or even more, for future use.

Basic Sponge Cake

Measure the ingredients very carefully to get a perfect sponge! Use this cake for Hawaiian cake or a Blackforest cake for which the variation in the recipe is given.

Makes 8-10 slices

4 large eggs
115 gm (2/3 cup plus 1 tbsp) powdered sugar
85 gm (½ cup plus 2 tbsp) flour (maida)
1 tsp baking powder, 1½ tbsp hot water, 1½ tsp vanilla essence

1. Separate white and yellow of eggs.
2. Beat egg whites till stiff.
3. Add sugar gradually (2 tbsp at a time) & keep beating till all the sugar is used up.
4. Add yolks. Mix well. Add essence.
5. Add boiling water, half tbsp at a time and beat more. Beat till the mixture of eggs and sugar is thick, frothy and three times in volume.
6. Sift maida with baking powder.
7. Fold in maida using a spoon (not a beater) adding half of it at a time.
8. Put in a greased and dusted tin of 9" diametre and bake for 30-35 minutes in a preheated oven at 180°C/350°F.
9. When the sponge cake leaves or shrinks away from the sides of the tin, it is done. The top of the cake is springy to touch and the cake springs back when touched lightly with a finger.
10. Now, insert a knife or skewer in the centre, only if the cake springs back and does not form a depression, when touched lightly with a finger. If the knife comes out clean, the cake is done. Remove from the oven.

VARIATIONS

CHOCOLATE SPONGE CAKE & PINEAPPLE SPONGE CAKE

For chocolate cake, add 4 tbsp cocoa powder and remove 4 tbsp flour from the measured quantity of flour and follow the above recipe. For pineapple cake, add 1 tsp of pineapple essence and 1 tsp of vanilla instead of 1½ tsp of vanilla essence and do as above.

Note: There are certain points to remember while mixing maida to the *eggs*.

1. While adding maida to the beaten eggs, sprinkle maida all over the eggs and not in one place. The eggs tend to sink because of the weight.
2. Always fold the maida, never beat. So never make a rotatory motion with the spoon while mixing maida. Always make a downward and upward movement with the spoon. Always handle the cake mixture gently.

Black Forest Cake

Picture on facing page & 79   Serves 12

4 egg chocolate sponge cake - page 97
1 cup tinned cherries
1 tbsp rum or few drops of brandy essence - optional
1 dark milk chocolate (40 gms) - for the flakes

CREAM ICING
250 gms cream - chilled
5 tbsp powdered sugar
1 tsp of vanilla essence

1. Prepare a chocolate sponge cake as given on page 97. Cool the cake.
2. Keep the milk chocolate with the wrapper, on the outer surface of a hot oven so that it melts slightly & becomes soft.
3. Cool it in the fridge but do not make it very hard.
4. With the help of a potato-peeler, start peeling the back side of the chocolate on to a plate. Lovely flakes will be ready. These should be hardened by keeping in the freezer for half an hour.
5. Keep cream in a small pan in the freezer for about half an hour.
6. When the cream as well as the pan is properly chilled, add sugar and essence.
7. Beat carefully till the cream is thick and can stand in soft peaks. Put some in an icing gun and keep in the fridge. Keep the rest of the cream also in the fridge.
8. Remove seeds from the cherries, keeping aside a few.
9. Add rum or essence to ½ cup cherry syrup.
10. Cut the cake into two halves. Soak both halves with cherry syrup. About 4-5 tbsp of syrup only, are put on each piece of cake.
11. Spread 2 tbsp of cream icing on each piece of cake.
12. Put deseeded cherries on the cream on one piece and cover these with the other piece of cake.
13. Cover the cake completely with cream on all sides and the top.
14. Level top and sides with a broad knife dipped in chilled water.
15. Make a border on the edge by piping swirls of cream from the icing gun. Place a cherry on each swirl. Put flakes in the center. Keep in the fridge.

Note: The left over tinned cherries can be stored in a plastic or stainless steel box in the freezer compartment of the refrigerator for over a month.

Calzone : Recipe on page 62 ➤

Corn & Mushroom Quiche : Recipe on page 64, Black Forest Cake ➤

COOKIES, PIES, TARTS

&

SWEET SNACKS

A 9" flan tin with a loose (removable) bottom

A baking tray. Cover the back of this tray with aluminium foil and grease it. Baking the cookies on the flat backside makes it very convenient to handle the cookies when they are done.

Drop spoonfuls of mixture to get beautiful walnut and raisin cookies.

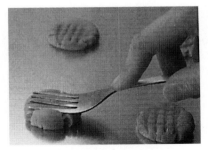

To flatten cookies use a fork to get a criss-cross design.

Walnut Brownies

Makes 10 *Picture on page 79*

½ cup (100 gm) butter
1¼ cups (175 gm) brown sugar
2 eggs
1 tsp vanilla essence or rum
½ cup (60 gm) flour (maida)
¼ tsp baking powder
½ cup cocoa powder
¾ cup (75 gm) walnuts - crushed into small pieces

1. Melt butter on low heat. Add brown sugar mix with wooden spoon till well mixed.
2. Add one egg. Mix well. Add the second egg and mix again
3. Add 1 tsp of vanilla essence or 1 tsp of rum
4. Sift flour, baking powder and cocoa together.
5. Keeping aside 2 tbsp walnuts for the topping, add the rest to the maida and mix well. Fold the flour and walnuts in the butter mixture.
6. Transfer to a medium sized greased tray or 8" square tin to get 1" thick layer of the mixture. Put walnut halves at intervals. Bake for atleast ½ hour on 180°C or till done. Cool and cut into square pieces.

Chocolate Chip Cookies

Makes 20-25

170 gms plain flour
120 gms butter, 55 gms sugar
3-4 tbsp chocolate pieces - roughly chopped
1 tsp vanilla essence

1. Beat the butter and sugar very well until light and creamy.
2. Add the vanilla essence and beat again.
3. Sieve the flour very well.
4. Add the flour and chocolate pieces. Gently mix in the flour and chocolate pieces to get a soft dough.
5. Shape into small round. Flatten slightly.
6. Cover the back of a baking tray with aluminium foil and grease it with butter. Place balls 1" apart. Bake in a preheated oven at 180°C/350°F for 15-20 minutes.

Walnut & Raisin Cookies

Picture on cover   *Makes 18-20*

¼ cup walnuts - crushed
¼ cup raisins (kishmish)
¼ cup desiccated coconut
½ cup flour (maida), 1 tsp baking powder
¼ cup butter - softened, ¼ cup powdered sugar
1 egg
½ tsp vanilla essence

1. Beat sugar and butter till fluffy. Add the egg and essence. Beat well till mixed.
2. Sift flour with baking powder. Add flour, walnuts and raisins. Mix gently.
3. Cover the back of a baking tray with aluminium foil and grease it with butter.
4. Put a spoonful of the batter on the prepared baking tray, 1" apart, to get irregular cookies as shown on page 100. Flatten slightly.
5. Bake for 20 minutes in a preheated oven at 160°C/325°F/Gas mark 3 or till golden brown. Cool and store in an airtight box.

Coconut Macaroons

Makes 16-20 macaroons

2 eggs whites
1 cup powdered sugar
1½ cups desiccated coconut
1 tsp vanilla essence
a pinch of salt

1. Whisk egg whites with a pinch of salt till stiff.
2. Fold in sugar, essence and coconut using a metal spoon to get a thick dropping batter.
3. Cover the back of a baking tray with aluminium foil and grease it with butter.
4. Put a spoonful of the batter on the prepared baking tray, 2" apart. Bake at 180°C/350°F/Gas mark 4 for 20-25 minutes or until light brown.
5. Cool on trays before removing from the tray.

Peanut Macaroons

Use crushed roasted peanuts instead of desiccated coconut to get peanut macaroons.

Cumin Cookies

Makes 16

120 gm flour (maida)
85 gm butter
20 gm sugar
½ tsp salt
½ tsp each of cumin seeds (jeera) and carom seeds (ajwain)

1. Preheat oven to 180°C.
2. Beat butter, sugar and salt well until light and creamy.
3. Sieve the flour. Add jeera and ajwain in it.
4. Add the flour to the butter mix. Gently mix to form a soft dough.
5. Form into small balls. Flatten slightly with a fork (as shown on page 100) and sprinkle a pinch of jeera or ajwain on it.
6. Line the back of a baking tray with aluminium foil. Grease the foil. Arrange biscuits on it, keeping them 1" apart. Bake for 15-20 minutes.
7. Remove cookies from the tray when slightly cold.

Cashewnut Cookies

Makes 15

100 gm maida (plain flour)
2 to 3 tbsp finely chopped cashewnuts
75 gm butter or margarine - softened
50 gm powdered sugar
2 to 3 drops almond essence or 1 tsp vanilla essence

1. Sieve the flour.
2. Preheat oven at 200°C/400°F.
3. Beat butter & sugar very well until light & creamy.
4. Add the essence and beat again.
5. Add the flour and mix gently to form a soft dough.
6. Form into small balls and roll into the chopped cashewnuts. Flatten slightly.
7. Arrange on a greased tray, keeping 1" apart.
8. Bake in a preheated oven for 15 to 20 minutes.
9. Remove from the tray when slightly cold.

Chocolate Sesame Cookies

Serves 15

60 gm plain flour (maida)
30 gm cocoa
75 gm butter - softened
60 gm powdered sugar
1 tsp vanilla essence
1 tsp sesame seeds (white til)

1. Cream butter and sugar till light and fluffy.
2. Add essence and beat again.
3. Sift flour and cocoa together.
4. Add flour to butter and mix gently to form a soft dough.
5. Form into balls. Sprinkle a pinch of sesame seeds on top. Bake in a preheated oven at 180°C for 13-15 minutes on a baking tray lined and greased with aluminium foil.

Note: If the dough feels too soft to form balls, keep it in the fridge but do not add any extra flour.

Chocolate Glace Cookies

Serves 15

CHOCOLATE GLACE ICING
1 tbsp cocoa
4-5 tbsp icing sugar
1 tsp warm water, approx.
½ tsp butter - softened

1. Prepare chocolate cookies as given above, but just omit the sesame seeds. Instead make a deep depression in each cookie with the thumb, before they are put in the oven, to make place for the icing drop.
2. For the icing, sift icing sugar. Put in small bowl.
3. Add cocoa. Add 1 tsp warm water and mix well to get a glossy icing of a thick pouring consistency.
4. Mix in white butter. Put icing with a spoon on the depression of the cooled cookies. Leave aside to set for 1 hour.

Fresh Fruit Tarts

Makes 8   *Picture on page 49*

TART SHELLS (SHORT CRUST PASTRY DOUGH)
120 gm (1 cup) plain flour (maida)
60 gm (¼ cup) salted butter - cold
a pinch baking powder, 1 tbsp powdered sugar
2-3 tbsp ice cold water

SUGAR SYRUP
1 cup water, 2 tbsp sugar, 1 tsp lemon juice
1 tsp cornflour, ½ tsp butter - softened

CUSTARD FILLING
2½ tbsp custard powder, 1 cup milk, 2 tbsp sugar

MIXED FRUITS - ALL CUT NEATLY INTO MEDIUM PIECES
1 slice pineapple, 1 nashpati (pear)
1 chiku, 1 kiwi, a few strawberries, 1 orange, a few grapes or fresh anaar ke dane
a few glace cherries

1. Cut the cold, solid butter into small pieces.
2. Add baking powder, sugar and butter to the flour. Rub the butter into the flour with the finger tips till it resembles bread crumbs.
3. Add 2-3 tbsp cold water. Bind into a dough of rolling consistency. Knead lightly.
4. Roll out large chappati of 1/8" thickness. Cut out small circles with a biscuit cutter or katori, which is slightly bigger than the tart mould and fit them into tart tins. Prick with a fork. Bake blind for 8 minutes in the centre of a hot oven 200°C till very light golden in colour. Take out from oven. Cool.
5. Prepare sugar syrup by boiling 1 cup water, 2 tbsp sugar and 1 tsp lemon juice. After it comes to a boil, let it boil for 2-3 minutes. Add hard fruits like nashpati and pineapple. Remove from fire and cool for 2 minutes. Add the soft fruits like kiwi, chiku and grapes. Strain after 5 minutes.
6. To the strained sugar syrup, add cornflour and butter. Cook on fire, stirring all the time till the sauce coats the back of the spoon. Remove from fire and keep the glazing aside.
7. In a clean, kadhai, mix custard powder, milk and sugar. Cook stirring till very thick and lumpy. Cool.
8. Fill cooled tart shells with thick custard. Top with neatly arranged fruits. Arrange a piece of glace cherry. Spoon glazing (cornflour sauce) over the arranged fruits in the tart. Serve after some time at room temperature or cold.

Apple Roll

Picture on page 79   *Makes 2 Rolls, Serves 8*

FILLING
250 gm apples (2 medium) - peeled and cut into tiny pieces
½ tsp cinnamon (dalchini) powder
1-2 tbsp chopped cashews

WRAP
¾ cup flour (maida)
½ tsp baking powder
3 tbsp butter - softened

SUGAR SYRUP TO BASTE
¾ cup sugar
1 cup water
1 tbsp butter

1. For the wrap, sift the flour and baking powder together. Rub in 3 tbsp butter with the finger tips. Add enough ice cold water to make a dough. Keep covered in the refrigerator.
2. For the filling, peel, core and cut the apples into small pieces and sprinkle with cinnamon powder. Mix cashews. Keep aside.
3. Boil sugar with water to make the syrup. After the first boil, keep boiling on low heat for about 4-5 minutes. Remove from fire and add 1 tbsp butter.
4. Divide the dough into 2 balls. Roll each ball into a rectangle.
5. Spread half the apple mixture over the dough and roll it like a swiss roll. Prepare the other roll also in the same way.
6. Put the rolls in a greased baking tray and bake in a moderate oven at 180°C/350°F/Gas mark 4 for 1 hour. Baste the roll every 15 minutes inbetween with sugar syrup while baking.
7. Cut into slices. Serve plain or with custard or cream.

Choco Truffle Tarts

Makes 10

3-4 tbsp chopped walnuts

SHORT CRUST PASTRY (DOUGH) FOR TART SHELLS
200 gm maida (plain flour)
100 gm salted butter - cold
a big pinch (1/8 tsp) baking powder
2 tbsp powdered sugar
3-4 tbsp ice cold water

CHOCOLATE BUTTER ICING
1½ cups white butter - softened
1½ cups powdered sugar - sifted
½ cup cocoa, can add more if desired
1 tsp vanilla essence

TRUFFLE FILLING
120 gm chocolate (3 slabs) - softened
50 gm (¼ cup) cream

1. Make the tart shells as given for lemon tarts on page 120. Keep aside to cool.
2. To prepare the chocolate butter icing, whip butter till smooth. Mix all the other ingredients and beat till well blended. Transfer to a piping bag and keep in the refrigerator.
3. For the truffle filling, break chocolate slabs into small pieces and melt in a heavy bottomed nonstick pan or in a microwave.
4. When the chocolate melts, add cream on low heat. Cook for 2 minutes, stirring continuously on low heat. You may add the cream on low power if using the microwave. Do not let it boil. Remove from heat and cool to room temperature.
5. To fill the tart shell, pipe chocolate butter icing at the edges, along the tart shell. Drop a spoonful of truffle filling in the centre to fill the empty space. Sprinkle some chopped walnuts on the sides. Refrigerate till serving time.

Date & Walnut Pie

Picture on facing page   *Serves 8*

SHORT CRUST PASTRY
**300 gms (2½ cups approx.) flour (maida), ¼ tsp baking powder
150 gms salted butter - cold and solid, 2 tbsp powder sugar
4-5 tbsp ice cold water to bind
loose bottomed flan tin of 9" diameter**

FILLING
**400 gm dates - stoned and chopped finely
¾ cup water, 2 tbsp lemon juice, 1 tbsp butter
1 cup chopped walnuts, ½ tsp vanilla essence, ½ cup cream**

1. For the short crust pastry, cut cold butter into tiny cubes.
2. Sift flour with baking powder. In a blender put half the flour. Add half the butter. Again put the left over flour and then the left over butter. Churn for a few seconds. Scrape the sides with a spatula or a knife and churn again for a few seconds only. Do not churn the mixer too much. Transfer to a mixing bowl and mix lightly.
3. Add just enough ice cold water to bind. Knead very lightly without pressure to form a dough. Wrap in a damp cloth and keep in the fridge for atleast 30 minutes to get cold, otherwise it becomes difficult to roll.
4. For the filling, mix dates, water, lemon juice and water. Heat on slow fire, for about 3-4 minutes, till pulpy. Remove from fire. Add cream and essence. Add walnuts, keeping aside a few for the topping.
5. To make the pie, keeping aside a 1/3 of the dough, roll out the rest on a flat work table, so that it is ¼" thick and 4" bigger in diameter than the flan tin (see page 64) or the pie dish, such that it covers the base & sides of the tin or pie dish. If you find it difficult to roll it, place the dough in the tin and spread it out to cover the bottom and sides. Trim off the excess by rolling a rolling pin on the edges.
6. Prick the base lightly with a fork. Bake at 200°C in a preheated oven for 15 minutes or till pastry shell turns golden yellow. Remove from oven.
7. After it cools down, arrange the filling over it. Level it.
8. Roll out the left over pastry very thinly and cut into thin strips. Arrange in a crisscross fashion on the pie and arrange walnuts. Bake further for 15 minutes. Serve hot with vanilla ice cream or fresh cream.

Chocolate Temptation : Recipe on page 94, Date & Walnut Pie ➤

Apple Short Cake

Cake mixture sandwiched with apples and then baked. Cut it into wedges to serve.

Serves 8

APPLE MIXTURE
500 gm (3 medium) apples - peel and cut into small pieces
¼ cup sugar
1 tsp lemon juice
½ tsp cinnamon powder
2 tbsp chopped almonds or cashews
1 tsp lemon rind (grate a whole lemon gently on the grater, turning around to get the yellow peel without the white pith)

CAKE DOUGH
½ cup (125 gm) butter
1 cup powdered sugar
1 egg
1½ cups flour (maida)
1 tsp baking powder

1. Cook apples with lemon juice and sugar till tender and dry. Remove from fire and add cinnamon powder, nuts and lemon rind. Keep aside.
2. For the cake, sift flour with baking powder.
3. Beat butter and sugar lightly. Add egg and beat well till frothy.
4. Mix in the flour to get a soft dough. Mix till smooth.
5. Divide dough into 2 balls.
6. Roll out one ball between 2 plastic sheets to the size of the cake tin.
7. Grease and dust the cake tin of about 8" diametre. Fit the rolled out dough into the prepared tin.
8. Spread the apple mixture on it.
9. Roll out the second ball and carefully place it on the apples.
10. Press the edges together & brush with water. Sprinkle 1 tsp of sugar on the cake.
11. Bake at 180°C for about 40 minutes or till done.
12. Allow to stand for 15 minutes before removing from the tin.

Swiss Rolls with Chocolate

Servings 12

FOR THE CAKE
1 baking tray - size 9"x11" approx.
4 large eggs
10 level tbsp flour (maida), 10 level tbsp powdered sugar
2 level tsp baking powder
1 tsp vanilla essence

CHOCOLATE FILLING
½ cup white butter - softened
¾ cup powdered sugar - sifted, ¼ cup cocoa, approx.
1 tsp vanilla essence

1. Separate white and yolk of eggs.
2. Beat egg whites in a dry pan, till stiff.
3. Add sugar gradually, beating after each addition. Add essence.
4. Sift maida with baking powder.
5. Add maida to eggs & fold with a spoon.
6. Pour into a greased and dusted rectangular baking tray and bake for 15 minutes in a preheated oven at 200°C.
7. When the cake leaves the sides of the tray and is springy to touch, remove from the oven. Spread powdered sugar on a grease proof paper and turn out the cake over the sugar.
8. To prepare the filling, sift sugar & cocoa powder. In a pan put butter. Beat till fluffy. Add all the other ingredients and beat well till well mixed. (Add more cocoa and sugar, according to your taste.)
9. Spread the chocolate filling and roll upwards. See pictures.
10. Pack the roll tightly in a plastic wrap or aluminium foil and keep in the fridge till required. To serve, cut the roll into 14-15 pieces.

BAKED
DESSERTS & PUDDINGS

Baked Pineapple
with Fruity Caramel Sauce

Enjoy it by itself or topped with some ice cream.
Serves 5-6

1 fresh, ripe pineapple
1 tbsp butter - softened
3 tbsp sugar

BLEND TOGETHER
1 large mango - peeled and chopped
1 banana
½" piece soft ginger - grated

OTHER INGREDIENTS
½ cup sugar - to caramelize
½ of a family pack of vanilla ice cream
10 almonds - cut into thin long pieces, for decoration

1. Peel the pineapple and cut into rings of ¼-½" thickness. Cut ring into 2 pieces and remove the hard core. Chop into 1" pieces. Heat 1 tbsp butter in a pan. Add pineapple and 2 tbsp sugar. Mix well for a few seconds only to coat them with butter. Remove from fire.

2. Place the buttered pineapple in a shallow oven-proof dish. Sprinkle 1 tbsp sugar over it. Heat oven to 175°C and place the pineapple in it and bake for   25-30 minutes. Remove from oven.

3. To prepare the sauce, place peeled and chopped mango, peeled banana and grated ginger in a blender and blend to a smooth puree. Keep aside. (The puree should be 1½ cups).

4. For the sauce, heat a thick bottomed kadhai. Add ½ cup sugar. Stir on low heat till the sugar just turns golden yellow in colour. Let it be yellow and not brown. Remove from fire. Do not over cook or bring to a boil, it will make the sauce dark & bitter. Add the pureed fruit and mix well. Stir continuously on low heat for a few minutes till the puree blends well with caramel. Remove from heat.

5. Pour the fruity caramel sauce over the baked pineapples. Sprinkle almonds. Bake again at 175°C for 10-15 minutes. Remove. Serve warm or cold, topped with scoops of vanilla ice cream.

Hot Chocolate Souffle

Serve it straight from the oven. Do not open the oven door till the baking time is complete. The souffle tends to sink very fast, so to avoid this, work upto step 5 and prepare the custard, but add the eggwhites and bake only 30 minutes (it's baking time) before serving. The bowls are greased with butter and sprinkled with sugar which help the souffle climb up the dish firmly!

Picture on back cover   Serves 6

1/3 cup cocoa
¾ cup powdered sugar
1 cup milk
2 tbsp cornflour dissolved in 2 tbsp milk
1 tbsp butter - softened
3 eggs
½ tsp vanilla essence

1. Grease small bowls or a dish with butter and then sprinkle sugar on the sides.
2. Mix sugar and cocoa with milk. Bring to a boil.
3. Add the cornflour paste, stirring continuously.
4. Mix the butter. Remove from fire. Cool and add essence.
5. Add beaten egg yolk one at a time. Keep aside till serving time.
6. Half an hour before serving, beat the egg whites till stiff.
7. Fold the stiff egg whites into the chocolate mixture.
8. Pour the mixture into the prepared bowls or dish, filling it ¾ height. Bake at 180°C/350°F/Gas mark 4 for 30 minutes. Serve immediately.

Blue Berry Cheese Cake

Cheese cakes are now very popular, so I thought of including this cake even though only the base is of a sponge cake and the rest of the cake is chilled.

Serves 8   *Picture on page 1*

BASE
1 basic sponge cake - recipe on page 97

CHEESE CAKE
500 gm cream
½ cup plus 2 tbsp powdered sugar
4 tbsp level cheese spread
5-6 tbsp blue berry jam - beat till smooth (see note)
4 tsp gelatine

TOPPING
2 tbsp blue berry jam
2-3 biscuits, preferably good day - crushed, a few black grapes

1. Bake a sponge cake as given on page 97. Cut the cake horizontally to get 1" thick cake. Press this cake with a rolling pin (belan). Fit it into a 8" flan tin. (A loose bottomed cake tin)
2. To prepare the cheese cake, whip cream till slightly thick.
3. Separately beat cheese spread with sugar in a big pan till smooth.
4. Add the whipped cream to it. Beat well till mixed properly.
5. Melt gelatine in ¼ cup water on low heat till it dissolves. Remove from fire. Add jam to it and mix well.
6. Very gradually, add the hot gelatine and jam in very small amounts into the cream mixture, stirring immediately with the other hand to mix the gelatine into the mixture well. Check sugar and add a little more if required.
7. Pour on the cake. Chill till set.
8. For the topping, beat jam lightly. Put a round blob of jam, about 2"-3" diameter in the center.
9. Arrange black grapes in a heap in the center. Make a 1" border of crushed biscuits or whipped cream. Cover with a cling film. Refrigerate till set. Remove from the tin along with the base of the tin.

Note: If blueberry jam is unavailable, try cooking 250 gm (2 cups) black grapes with ¼ cup sugar and 1 tbsp water. Boil. Simmer on low flame till grapes get soft, for about 5-7 minutes. Remove from fire and cool. Blend in a mixer and use instead of jam. You can also use an eggless cake and make the dessert eggless.

Crumb Delight with Rum

A delicious pudding made with biscuit crumbs. If you do not feel like adding rum, soak the raisins in milk instead. Serve it plain or with ice cream or cream.

Serves 8

2 cups coarsely crushed Marie biscuits (1 big pack plus a few extra)
2 eggs - separated
1/3 cup powdered sugar
¼ cup butter - softened
1 tsp baking powder
1 tsp vanilla essence
½ cup crushed walnuts
¼ cup raisins (kishmish), preferably black raisins - soaked in 3 tbsp rum
2-3 tbsp milk

1. Put biscuits in a polythene and crush with a rolling pin (belan).
2. Beat sugar and butter till creamy.
3. Add the baking powder, essence, nuts, crushed biscuits and raisins along with the rum. Mix well.
4. Add the egg yolks.
5. Beat the whites stiff and add to the batter.
6. Add milk to make the batter softer.
7. Pour into a greased oven proof serving dish and bake for 25-30 minutes at 160°C/325°F/Gas mark 3.
8. Serve plain or with cream or ice cream or with chocolate sauce.

Baked Guavas with Cream

Whole guavas are baked and filled with cream. If you like, you can fill them with an interesting flavour of ice cream too.

Serves 6

6 medium fresh, ripe guavas of good quality
6 tsp sugar
250 gm cream
3-4 drops vanilla essence
6 tbsp powdered sugar
2 tbsp finely chopped cashewnuts
3 glace cherries

1. Peel guavas. Slice off an ½" thick piece from the top. Scoop out the seeds with a spoon or a scooper.
2. Sprinkle 1 tsp of sugar inside each guava and spread it nicely on the inner surface with a spoon.
3. Bake in a preheated oven at 200°C for about 15-20 minutes till they become soft. Do not let them become limp by being in the oven for a longer time.
4. Cool. Keep in the fridge.
5. Beat cream with sugar and essence till soft peaks are formed. Fill some cream in an icing bag for decoration, if desired.
6. Mix nuts in the left over beaten cream very gently. Chill.
7. Fill guavas with cream mixed with nuts. Top with a swirl of beaten cream in the icing gun. Decorate with half a cherry. Refrigerate.
8. Serve on a bed of thin cream in a low sided dish.

Sticky Toffee Pudding

Bake it in a serving dish and serve it straight from there with cream, custard sauce or just by itself. You can also serve it warm during winters with ice cream.

Serves 8

2 cups flour (maida)
200 gm dates - pitted (seed removed) and chopped (1 cup)
1½ cups boiling water
1 tsp baking soda-bi-carb
1 tsp baking powder
75 gm (¼ cup plus 2 tbsp) butter - softened
1 cup powdered sugar
2 eggs
1 tsp vanilla essence

TOFFEE TOPPING
½ cup brown sugar
60 gm (¼ cup) butter
2 tbsp cream

1. Mix dates, soda-bi-carb and boiling water, let it stand for 15 minutes.
2. Beat the butter until creamy. Beat in the sugar.
3. Add the egg and the essence. Beat very well.
4. Sift flour and baking powder. Add to the above mixture and mix well.
5. Add the date mixture along with the water in which they are soaked.
6. Pour into a large greased oven proof shallow glass dish. (A rectangular borosil dish looks good.)
7. Bake in a preheated oven at 180°C/350°F/Gas mark 4 for 40 minutes or until done. Prick with a fork.
8. In a heavy bottomed sauce pan, cook the remaining butter and the brown sugar on low heat till sugar melts. Remove from fire. Add cream and mix.
9. Spread the brown sugar mixture on to the pudding and put under the grill or at 220° C for 3 minutes.
10. Cool and serve with cream.

Black Currant Pudding

A crunchy bread pudding.

Serves 6-8

6 slices of brown bread - buttered and spread with jam (black currant preferably) or orange marmalade or any one of your choice

MIX TOGETHER
4 tbsp kellogs cornflakes
2 tbsp melted butter
2 tbsp powdered sugar

FILLING
4 pears or 2 apples - peeled and cut into four and then into thin slices
¼ tsp cinnamon (dalchini) powder
1 tsp lemon juice
1 tbsp kishmish - soaked in water
2 tbsp brown sugar
8-10 almonds - sliced
5-6 glace cherries - sliced thinly

CUSTARD
2 cups milk
2 tbsp sugar
2 tbsp cornflour
1 tsp vanilla essence

1. Remove sides of bread and cut into thin long fingers.
2. Arrange fingers of 3 slices in a medium sized oven proof dish.
3. Sprinkle half the cornflakes mixed with butter and sugar over it.
4. Mix some lemon juice and dalchini powder to the fruit. Arrange half of the fruit slices and kishmish on the cornflakes.
5. Sprinkle some brown sugar on top.
6. Repeat the layer of bread fingers, cornflakes and the left over fruit and kishmish.
7. Dissolve cornflour in ¼ cup milk. Boil left over milk with sugar. Add cornflour paste and cook till a thick custard of pouring consistency is ready. Add essence.
8. Pour the custard over the fruit.
9. Top with sliced almonds and glace cherries.
10. Bake in a moderate oven for about 20 minutes or till golden. Serve hot.

Apple Crumble

Serves 8-10

TOPPING
2 cups flour (maida)
1 tsp baking powder
1 cup powdered sugar
½ cup butter

APPLE LAYER
8 apples (1½ kg) - peeled and cut into slices
2 tbsp lemon juice (juice of 1 lemon)
1 tsp powdered cinnamon (dalchini)
½ cup sugar

1. Sieve the flour and baking powder.
2. Add the powdered sugar.
3. Cut the butter into small pieces. Rub butter in the flour with your finger tips till the mixture resembles fine bread crumbs. Keep aside.
4. Peel and slice the apples. Add lemon juice. Add ½ cup sugar and the cinnamon powder. Cook for 5 minutes till apples are slightly tender. Do not mash the slices.
5. Arrange the apple slices in a glass baking dish.
6. Spread the flour mixture. Press gently.
7. Bake in a preheated oven for 30-40 minutes or until slightly golden. Serve with ice cream or whipped cream.

Orange & Pineapple Meringues

Serves 6

6 oranges, 1 small tin pineapple slices
3 eggs
1 tbsp butter - softened
6 tbsp powdered sugar

1. Cut the oranges in half, carefully remove the flesh and reserve the shells.
2. Skin orange segments. Chop the pineapple pieces and the orange flesh.
3. Separate the eggs. Beat the yolks with the butter and 3 tbsp powdered sugar.
4. Add the pineapple and orange to the yolk mixture.
5. Pour the mixture in the orange shells. Keep aside till serving time.
6. Just before serving, beat the egg whites till stiff and then add the left over 3 tbsp of the sugar.
7. Spoon the egg white over the orange shells.
8. Bake in a preheated oven at 230°C/450°F/Gas mark 8 for 5-7 minutes.

Bread Pudding

Serves 6

4 bread slices - toasted, sides removed and buttered
2 eggs - beat well
1½ cups milk, ¼ cup sugar
1 tsp vanilla essence
¼ cup mixture of chopped nuts and raisins

1. Cut bread into triangles and arrange in a buttered pie dish and sprinkle with nuts.
2. Heat milk and sugar, just enough to dissolve the sugar. Remove from fire and add the eggs and vanilla essence.
3. Strain the mixture into the pie dish.
4. Bake at 180°C/350°F/Gas mark 4 for 45 minutes or until pudding is set with a firm crusty top. Serve hot from the dish.

Baked Cheese Cake
with Vanilla Sauce

Serves 8

½ kg paneer - grated finely
1 tin (400 gm) milk maid (condensed milk)
1½ tsp baking powder, 1½ tsp soda-bi-carb (mitha soda)
½ cup melted butter, 1 tsp vanilla essence
½ cup almonds - ground to a rough powder
4 tbsp kishmish - soaked in warm water and drained, 2 tbsp flour (maida)
2-3 tbsp milk

TO DECORATE
chiku or kiwi or any fresh seasonal fruit - cut into thin slices
some fresh or tinned cherries, grapes, orange, some powdered sugar to dust

VANILLA SAUCE
½ cup milk mixed with 1 tsp cornflour
2 tsp sugar, ½ cup cream, 1 tsp vanilla essence

1. Preheat oven to 150°C. Grease and dust with flour, an 8" loose bottomed tin.
2. Beat paneer and condensed milk till well mixed.
3. Add baking powder and soda-bi-carb. Beat well again.
4. Add melted butter, ground almonds and essence. Mix well.
5. Add 2 tbsp flour to kishmish. Mix well and add to the cake mixture. Mix. Add 2-3 tbsp of milk if the mixture appears too thick. The batter should be of a thick dropping consistency.
6. Transfer the mixture to the prepared tin. Bake in the preheated oven for 40 minutes until firm and slightly shrunken from the sides of the tin.
7. Check with a clean knife or a toothpick. If done switch off the heat and leave cheesecake inside to cool completely.
8. To serve, remove cheesecake from tin and top with thin slices of any seasonal fruit. Make a border of halved kiwi slices or any fruit of your choice. Open an orange segment in the centre and top it with cherries or grapes. Dust with icing sugar. Serve at room temperature or chilled with vanilla sauce or with chocolate sauce served separately in a small milk pot or with ice cream.
9. To prepare the vanilla sauce, mix milk with cornflour and sugar. Keep on fire and stir till it turns thick and coats the spoon. Remove from fire and let it cool. Add essence and cream. Chill in the refrigerator in a small milk pot.

Um Ali

Made in Arabic households during Eid, the literal translation means mother of Ali. About a cup of mixed nuts & raisins is used in the recipe, so in the absence of any one, just make up the total quantity to about a cup.

Serves 8

¼ cup pistachio nuts - chopped
¼ cup almonds - chopped
¼ cup walnuts - chopped
3-4 tbsp raisins (kishmish)
2 ripe bananas - peeled and sliced thinly
¼ cup plus 2 tbsp sugar
2 cups milk
seeds of 5 cardamoms (chhoti illaichi) - crushed
2-3 threads saffron (kesar)
4 slices bread - toasted and sides removed
½ cup cream - whipped till thick

1. Keeping aside a few nuts for the top, add the rest of the nuts, raisins, bananas and sugar to the milk.
2. Add saffron and cardamoms also to the milk. Bring to a boil. Boil for 10 minutes.
3. Grease a baking dish with butter. Arrange toasted bread to cover the base of the dish.
4. After the milk has been boiling for 30 minutes, remove from fire. Strain the nuts and bananas from the milk.
5. Arrange the nuts and fruit on the bread in the dish.
6. Cool the milk and add whipped cream to it. Check sugar. Add 1-2 tbsp powdered sugar, if required
7. Pour the milk and whipped cream mixed together over the nuts and bananas.
8. Bake for 20 minutes at 180°C/350°F/Gas mark 4.
9. Top with nuts and serve.

Striped Chocolate Cheese Cake

A beautiful white and chocolate striped cheese cake. Only the base is baked whereas the cheese cake is set in the refrigerator.

Serves 8

BISCUIT BASE
100 gms Marie biscuits (1 small pack)
1/3 cup melted butter
2 tbsp milk

CHEESE CAKE
3 cups curd - hang for 2 hours
125 gm butter (½ cup) - softened
1¼ cups powdered sugar
3 tbsp gelatine, 2 tsp lemon juice
1 slab (of 40 gm) chocolate, preferably dark - at room temperature

1. Crush the biscuits with a rolling pin.
2. Mix in the melted butter with finger tips and add 2 tbsp milk.
3. Press into the base of an 8" loose bottomed cake tin.
4. Bake in a preheated oven at 180°C/ 350°F/Gas mark 4 for 10 minutes.
5. Hang the curd for 2 hours in a muslin cloth.
6. Beat butter till smooth. Add hung curd and sugar. Beat well.
7. Soak the gelatine in ¼ cup water mixed with 2 tsp lemon juice. Heat on a low fire until dissolved.
8. Add gelatine gradually to the curd mixture, stirring well after each addition. Mix well.
9. Divide the mixture into two parts.

The loose bottom tin allows you to unmould the cheese cake with the biscuit base intact. Press the buttered crumbs evenly and firmly onto the bottom of the pan.

10. Break chocolate into small pieces. Add ¼ cup water and keep in a heavy bottomed pan on very low heat, stirring until melted properly. Add half of the melted chocolate to one cheese cake mixture, keeping the other mixture white.
11. Pour the chocolate curd mixture on the biscuit base in the tin. Keep the white mixture aside.

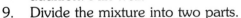

12. Chill chocolate cheese cake for ½ hour in the freezer to firm up.
13. Remove from freezer. Pour the remaining white mixture (whip it if it sets) on top of the chocolate mixture and now chill in the refrigerator. (do not keep in the freezer).
14. After 1 hour, when the top layer of the cheese cake is set, pour the left over melted chocolate over the cheese cake. Serve after 3-4 hours or after it is set.

Sponge Fruit Pudding

Serves 8

½ kg apples/pears/strawberries - cut into ½" pieces
¼ cup sugar
1/3 cup butter - softened
1/3 cup powdered sugar
1 cup flour (maida)
1 tsp baking powder
3 egg whites
4 tbsp milk
2 tbsp icing sugar - sieved

1. Cook the fruit with ¼ cup sugar, stirring gently, till slightly soft. Remove from fire.
2. Place the stewed fruits in a glass oven proof dish.
3. Beat the butter and powdered sugar until light and fluffy.
4. Sift flour with baking powder and fold in the sieved flour into the butter mixture.
5. Whisk the egg whites until stiff and gently fold into the creamed mixture.
6. Add milk to the cake mixture. Spread over the fruit.
7. Bake in a preheated oven at 180°C/350°F/Gas mark 4 for 40-50 minutes or until firm to touch. Remove from oven. Sprinkle icing sugar and serve with cream.

Peach Trifle

Picture on facing page

Serves 10

CHIFFON SPONGE CAKE
¼ cup flour (maida), ¼ cup cornflour
1 tsp baking powder, a pinch of salt
4 eggs
½ cup powdered sugar, 1 tsp vanilla essence

THICK CUSTARD FILLING
2¼ cups milk, 6 tbsp vanilla custard powder
6 tbsp sugar, ½ cup finely chopped peaches
1 tsp vanilla essence

TOPPING
1 tin peach halves, a few blanched almonds, cherries
a few chocolate thins (After 8 or any other chocolate) - cut into half diagonally

TO SOAK
½ cup syrup from the peach tin, 1 tbsp rum or brandy, optional

1. For the cake, sieve flour, cormflour, baking powder and salt.
2. Separate the eggs. Beat the egg whites till stiff. Add essence.
3. Add sugar to the egg whites and whisk till thick and smooth. Add the egg yolks.
4. Gently fold in the flour mixture into the eggs. Pour in a 8" greased and dusted cake tin. Bake in a preheated oven at 200°C/400°F/Gas mark 6 for 15 minutes.
5. For the custard filling, mix milk with sugar and custard powder in a heavy bottomed pan. Keep on fire, stirring continuously till it boils. Cook for about 5-7 minutes or till it turns very thick. Remove from fire and cool to room temperature. Add vanilla essence.
6. Cut the cake into 2 halves. Cool the cake to room temperature.
7. Place a piece of cake in a serving dish. Mix ½ cup peach syrup with brandy or rum if you are using. Soak cake with 4-5 tbsp of this peach syrup.
8. Keeping aside 4-5 tbsp custard for the top, spread the rest of the custard on soaked piece of cake. Spread the chopped pieces of peaches.
9. Soak the second piece of cake too with peach syrup and invert it on the custard.
10. Spread the remaining custard on top of the cake.
11. Cut each peach half into thin slices lengthwise to get thin long pieces. Arrange slices overlapping slightly to completely cover the top. Garnish with whipped cream, almonds and chocolates. Serve cold.

Chicken with Olives & Tomatoes : Recipe on page 14, Peach Trifle ➤

Nita Mehta's BEST SELLERS (Non-Vegetarian)

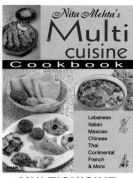

MULTICUISINE
Cookbook

THAI
cooking for the Indian kitchen

Dilli Ka Khaana

MEXICAN
cooking for the Indian kitch

SOUPS & SALADS

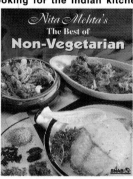

The Best of
Non-Vegetarian

LOW CALORIE
cooking for the Indian kitchen

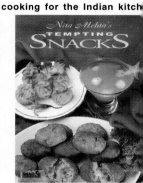

Tempting
SNACKS

CHINESE Cookery

Tikka Seekh & Kebab

OVEN Recipes
Non-Vegetarian

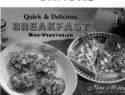

BREAKFAST
Non-Vegetarian

ITALIAN
Non-Vegetarian

Favourite Recipes

PUNJABI Cooking

CONTINENTAL
Non-Vegetarian

MUGHLAI
Non-Vegetarian

The Best of
CHICKEN Recipes

SNACKS
Non-Vegetarian

Favourite
NON-VEGETARIAN